TOM KENYON A

EDITED BY MARTINE VALLÉE

THE GREAT HUMAN POTENTIAL

WALKING IN ONE'S OWN LIGHT

Teaching from The Ninth Dimensional Pleiadians and The Hathors

www.ariane-books.com

Published by: Ariane Books
1217, av. Bernard O., suite 101, Outremont, Quebec, Canada H2V 1V7
Phone.: (1) 514-276-2949, Fax.: (1) 514-276-4121
info@editions-ariane.com — www.editions-ariane.com

Cover design : Carl Lemyre
Interior design : Kesse Soumahoro

ISBN : 978-2-89626-133-8

Distributed by: New Leaf
401 Thornton Rd. Lithia Springs, GA 30122-1557
Phone: 770.948.7845 —Fax: 770.944.2313
domestic@newleaf-dist.com —foreign@newleaf-dist.com.

Printed in Canada

Ariane online store
www.editions-ariane.com/boutique/

CONTENTS

INTRODUCTION
BY MARTINE VALLÉE

The greatest potential of all: Walking to the drum of your own light

Dear friends,

Even though my time as a full-time publisher for the French community was traded for work on more global issues, I still, once in a while, "pop in" for very special editorial projects. *The Great Human Potential* is one of them. Some of you may remember me from two previous books that were published in English: *The Great Shift and Transition Now*. To every one of you, I say, "*Welcome*."

Many times as I was preparing this book, I thought about the path that we all share and I sincerely think that one of the most precious moments in any human life is when one discovers its divine nature, when the journey back to source begins.

I remember clearly my own experience. It seemed so surreal that for awhile I felt as though I was walking on air. I instinctively knew that I had opened a door that was just waiting to be opened. I had entered a place where my higher consciousness lived and a whole new world was set into motion. My journey had just begun and I felt alive and free like never before. I'm sure many of you reading this know exactly what I am talking about.

These times are times of great acceleration and expansion, and if we really want to go from one reality to another, from one vibration to the next, we have to get serious about eliminating judgments, false beliefs and manipulations, especially those that come from religions. They are very powerful programs and they keep us in fear and drama, and when you have drama, you have karma. Another challenge is to understand that living in the moment is where all our potential is, not in the past, or the future. Usually, we ignore the present moment and, by doing so, we take away its power.

Right now, we are given the opportunity for a new scenario. We are advancing towards a completely different dispensation of consciousness, from the ego-conscience to the eco-conscience as written by Otto Sharmer in his book *Leading from the Emerging Future.* That higher level of consciousness will require the realization that we are not victims but rather willing participants. If we understand that we are the creators of 100% of our reality and accept it, then everything changes.

The ninth-dimensional Pleiadians say, "*...if you still see yourselves as victims, then you do not take responsibility for your part in the experience. You are judging and judgment is only possible in the mentality of victim/perpetrator.*"

With the passage of 2012, a new blueprint has been made available for each one of us. And this blueprint makes possible all potentials and available all realities. Furthermore, what is really "buzzing" and what we feel more and more is that, from now on, the changes that we want to see happening will not be only on the surface but will come from deep down. We have to go deep in our being, into our humanity, and see what we want to become, not only as an individual but as a community and a country. There is no more separation.

My purpose with this book is to bring you to live the highest version of your potential, and to do so, I have invited two groups that I find incredibly powerful and interesting: The Hathors channeled by Tom Kenyon and the Ninth-dimensional Pleiadians, channeled by Wendy Kennedy.

I must admit, I have a special place for what Wendy channels. With this particular group, I have finally understood the real nature of the illusion and how judgments and fears keep us in the illusion, and thus in the "game". They offer many solutions on how to integrate these judgments and fears so that we can all rewrite history, not only for ourselves but for humanity.

Then there is Tom Kenyon. Without a doubt, I consider Tom Kenyon and Judi amongst those people who had a big impact on my life. With Tom and the Hathors, I discovered the power of sound and these sounds have greatly participated in my spiritual evolution. Doors were opened that only sound can open. And no words could ever convey my immense gratitude for his work. With Judi by his side, they make a remarkable team and the year 2013 will mark the 25th anniversary of Tom's Egyptian alchemy exploration. What a fantastic journey!

In French, Tom channels two groups of Light beings: The Hathors and the Arcturians. Here you have only the part with the Hathors because Tom will be publishing himself the teachings of the Arcturians. It will be called *The Arcturian Anthology.* These teachings will be even more powerful with the addition of a sound CD and should be available in the fall of 2013. Do not miss it.

In closing, I simply want to say how grateful I am to every one of you who is taking the time to read this book. The path toward "home" is not a simple one, but if we find the courage to be our very own muse, to be the inspiration behind each of our creation, then we will walk tall to the drums of our own light. Is there a better place to be?

Finally, by taking responsibility for this spiritual journey, honoring our potential, and walking fully in our light, we recognize that each one of us has a role to play in the renaissance of our civilization. And that, dear reader, is the beginning of a brand new reality.

Have a great journey.

Martine Vallee
Montreal, August 2013
martine@passioncompassion.org

BOOK ONE OF POTENTIALS

The Ninth Dimensional Pleiadian Collective

The information that we give you in this book
is what we consider the most appropriate vibrational match
for where you are right now.

INTRODUCTION
FROM WENDY KENNEDY

In 1994, I began my adventures in channeling. After a year of working with my angelic guides and a few other higher dimensional beings through automatic writing, I was introduced to an amazing group of beings from the Pleiades who called themselves the Ninth Dimensional Pleiadian Collective. They had been patiently waiting for me to increase my frequency enough to begin to work with them verbally, not surprising since they work with tone and sound.

It has been an extraordinary journey with them. I cannot imagine what life would have been like without the support of these kind and loving beings. They encouraged and reminded me that I was capable of so much more than I was willing to allow myself to see or to be. In the thousands of private and group sessions I have done over the years with them, they have always offered encouragement to those seeking answers. Many times I would wonder how they would respond to someone's question when on the surface it seemed bleak. Never ones to sugar coat their answers, The Ps (as I affectionately call them) would always find a way of phrasing their replies so that an individual could see the service or growth potential in their choices, even the challenging ones the ego was not quite yet willing to release.

One of the perks of my "job" is that by working with so many different people, I get to see the general trends of what we are collectively processing. I have to admit that for the ego, it does make it a bit easier to relax and release issues when you know you aren't doing it alone and that everyone else is processing similar stuff. There is something within us that releases that illusion of separation and allows us to have more courage through the awareness of connection.

It is amazing to me how many have awakened in the last 20 years. I see what was once considered fringe as being mainstream, and I have no doubt that what is today considered a bit "out there" will be tomorrow's norm. With the passage of 2012, it now feels as if we have moved beyond many of the fears of destruction and the unknown and into a period of infinite possibility. I am truly honored to have been asked by Martine to contribute to this book, as I do believe we have so much potential, each of us, to create fascinating and wondrous things. It is just a matter of remembering that and allowing it to be our version of reality.

Wendy Kennedy

INTRODUCTION
FROM THE NINTH DIMENSIONAL PLEIADIAN COLLECTIVE

Greetings, Dears. This is the Ninth Dimensional Pleiadian Collective, and it is a pleasure and an honor to have the opportunity to connect with you. No matter when you are reading this, each and every time you think of us, we stand beside you. To us, we are always with you for it is always the next Now moment. Hmmm...we will let you think about that one for a bit. Perhaps it will make more sense to you as we share our perspective of time with you later.

What we present to you here is simply ***a version*** of the truth. It is not the only truth for there are infinite versions. The truth is always colored by perspective, that of the one telling the story and by those listening. But what we offer you is a stepping stone to your greater truth. Take the bits and pieces that resonate with you and leave the rest behind. You may be surprised if you read through this book several times that there may be whole sections you missed or couldn't comprehend and upon rereading them you had a newfound understanding. As your vibration changes, so will your perception.

We are so very excited to see what you create for yourselves, for this is the time of greatest potential on your planet. Each and every one of you has an amazing amount of support available to you, both in your world and "beyond the veil". Use it! Call on us. Know we always answer even if you cannot hear us. Move out of your head and into your heart for it is there we can be heard.

STELLAR HISTORY, WISDOM AND POTENTIAL

Let us begin by saying that through us, other beings are participating in this channeling and are very happy to share their perspective and wisdom about their star system.

To process the information that you are about to read, you must be in your heart center since the heart center doesn't have any of the distortions nor the beliefs that the mind has about your true history. Realize the history that you have been given, what was *sold* to you, was not your true history. As many of you know, for this grand experiment called planet Earth, your DNA was altered. We, from the Ninth Dimensional Pleiadian Collective, would like to give you a brief perspective on what it was all about and how it has brought you here to this point in time, allowing you to understand the past so that you can move towards your highest potential.

But first, we want to be honest here; we do have a different perspective than that of the White Brotherhood (with which many of your ascended masters align) about how to interact with you at this time. That doesn't mean that ours is right or wrong; it is just different.

The White Brotherhood and the ascended masters wish to work with you amongst the construct of the dimension within the illusion. We choose to be here and tell you about your galactic history, the illusion and the game that is being played, and how to move beyond it. We think that you are ready for a *new* story, another version of the truth. The White Brotherhood thinks that, for some of you, it will create too much of a shock, so information is released at a slower pace. Both perspectives serve you well. Everyone needs to work in a unique way, at their own pace. Some will align with what we are giving, others with the White Brotherhood, and many of you who are reading this understand both perspectives. Having different perspectives gives you the bigger picture and enables you to see different aspects of the experience.

Now, any information that you are receiving regardless of the source, be it an angelic guide, an ascended master or from us, take what resonates with you and leave the rest behind. Every being that you encounter will have an agenda. We have an agenda to support you, but also we are here to learn from you. We want to assist you in bringing in light and information. At the end of the day, you are your best authority. You always have the best answers for yourself.

The information that we give you in this book is what we consider the most appropriate vibrational match for where you are right now. For some of you, it may not resonate as much as for others. When we give information, we always look at the vibrational level of the majority of whom we think will be listening or reading this in order to give you a version of the truth that will best serve you in accessing your highest potential. In reality, there are infinite versions of the truth, and your vibration determines which version you experience. Another way for us to say that would be that you are constantly moving from Now moment to Now moment, stringing them together to experience different "timelines".

From time to time, we will say, "Take a deep breath". This small pause is there because we know that some of the information can be difficult for you to process. One of the ways many of you cope with difficult information or information that does not support the illusion of your reality is to leave your body—out you go! Your breath helps you to ground and connect again so that you may assimilate the information.

Earth and the Grand Experiment

Long ago, higher dimensional beings said, "Wouldn't it be fun to enter into density, forget who we are, and then try to get out of it? Wouldn't that be an interesting game?" So you all decided to do it. *YOU* were the ones that came up with the idea, and you are the very ones that are playing it out here on Earth.

There were two previous planetary experiments in the galaxy that tried to undergo the game of integration. They weren't successful in achieving it, but we did learn a great deal from them. When Earth was deemed suitable as a new experiment, it was then deposited with the genetic material from thousands and thousands of worlds. Along with the genetic material was all the emotional coding and experiences of these planets and species. We call Earth "The Planet of Emotion", and it is unlike any other planet in the entire Universe because your range of emotion is so vast. You have extreme highs and lows... and everything in between.

In other sectors of the galaxy, the emotional range is not as varied. This is in part why the two previous experiments did not go so well. When you lack emotional range, you have a far more focused existence. It means that your flexibility, your ability to pull in new ideas, new inspirations, and to be creative is somewhat limited. A focused existence does give you the opportunity to examine and explore reality in detail, but when it comes to the game of polarity integration, a wide variety of emotions and potential combinations allows for a higher probability of success. This process of integration includes, above all, letting go of judgment. It is the ability to see light and dark as an illusion, since both are part of source energy. You are once again unifying your perspective of light and dark to a complete, whole and divine state.

Earth itself is a living, ever-growing library complete with records of all the experiences of all consciousness on it. You have access to this library. Contrary to what you might feel, it is actually much, much easier for you to achieve integration on Earth since you have access to such a vast pool of genetic records and experiences. Again, remember, these experiences are not only from the beings and life forms that have lived on your planet, but also from the thousands of species who contributed their DNA to your world.

There are five seed races who donated their genetic material to create you, the modern human. We are talking about the Felines, the Reptilians, the Humanoids, the Avians (bird people) and higher dimensional Beings of Light from Lyra. This material was given so that you could have easier access to their records, giving you the greatest chance of succeeding in integration. Each of the five races has had diverse and extensive histories whose records give you knowledge and wisdom to pull from as you attempt integration. From their experiences, you can access information to glean insight into what may have helped or hindered the process of integration.

It is important for you to know this because this is the basic premise of your game. As you are going through this process of ascension and increasing your vibration rate, you are also completing a 26,000-year cycle. It is no coincidence that the two coincide. With the completion of this 26,000-year cycle, you are integrating everything that you have learned during this period. Think of a cycle like a running track with a start and finish line. This start/finish line is denoted in the galaxy by a band of extremely high-frequency energy. We called it the photonic band as it is composed of photon (or light) particles. These high vibrational particles of light assist and support you in elevating your frequency. Rather than remaining on the same track going around and around in circles, you actually spiral up with the completion of each cycle. As you near the end of a cycle, you are able to access once more everything that you've learned and then integrate it before moving on to the next. You began entering into this field of high vibratory light in the late 1980s and continue to move through it today. Most of humanity simply experiences this as life going faster and getting more hectic as their issues are more intensely reflected so they can clearly see where judgment needs to be released.

Take a few moments here... *to feel if the information we have shared has triggered any issues, such as manipulation, control or abandonment.*

You may also find it may have activated some level of homesickness. If this is the case, just take a nice, deep breath. Remember, always take what resonates and leave the rest behind. It is our version of history that we are sharing with you because we see that you are requesting it energetically, and we want you to move forward. Our purpose is to support you. Don't forget, the version of the story may change as you change, grow and expand.

We are sharing some bits and pieces of your true history, but the full picture will only be known and activated within each and every one of you when you are ready. When history is just given to you, it can be confusing and very hard to contemplate as there has been so much manipulation of information. At a certain point, you don't know who to trust. We are giving you a place to start so that each and every one of you can go within, to the Akashic records, and look at the histories and different genetic material available. You have simply forgotten that you have a library card. So take your card, go to the library, and see the librarian. Yes, there are beings that specialize in helping those of you who are looking for information. They are there to assist you. They will do their best to find the vibrational match to what you are looking for.

Not only are you at the end a 26,000-year cycle, but we are also at the end of a universal cycle. The end of this universal cycle has nothing to do with the counting of revolutions, but rather a result of the dissemination of information and skills that humanity gains and shares with the entire Universe. This new knowledge and wisdom will in essence change the universal game so dramatically that the game as it fundamentally exists can no longer be and is deemed complete. All this is accomplished through the holographic nature of the Universe.

Let us explain. As an individual, you are part of the whole. Every time an alteration is made to the whole, all the individual pieces are updated to reflect that change. If you make a change to any one of the individual pieces, all other pieces, as well as the whole itself, are also altered to mirror the change. So as you learn how to release judgment, you send out this information, the "how to go about it", to other aspects of yourselves, your genetic line, and all other beings in the Universe holographically. By doing that, you are changing the universal game because these other aspects now have access to new information that was previously unavailable until you experience it. Those lifetimes have the ability, if they so choose, to download and run the knowledge and wisdom you have shared through your life experience. It is quite exciting and powerful. This is one of the reasons that this is called "The Grand Experiment". Never before has a planet gone through the ascension process with conscious beings on it and with the emotional range that you have. That's why there is so much stellar and angelic support. We all understand how unique and transformative this experience is and will be.

We will say that there are other timelines on which this project or experience is not succeeding. But you, the version with which we are having this conversation, are successful, and you are going through the ascension process. There are infinite probabilities and ways to have experiences. Down here, where you are in the linear mindset, you think that there is only one version of reality that exists. But in actuality, there are multiple versions that are going on beside you and you are constantly moving at will, back and forth, between these versions as you adjust your frequency and vibration. But since you are processing reality through the mind, you think that you are only on one timeline. You still don't catch the fact that you have shifted. Occasionally, you will experience déjà vu, and that is an indication that you have shifted timelines. Your shift in perception, in beliefs and in frequency is usually pretty subtle since your version of reality doesn't change in a very dramatic way.

Even though you are not aware of your different timelines, your higher self always is. It is able to witness and participate in multiple versions of reality all at once. But the ego, this part of you that is having this limited existence, can't see it. That is a construct of the game. It is part of the beauty of this third dimension, feeling separate from the whole. It is at the same time unique and challenging, and it is what you came for.

As you go through this process of ascension, don't be in such a rush to get to the other side. You already know what that multidimensional experience is like! What you don't know, and what we are all learning from you, is how to go through this process of releasing judgment and by doing so mastering compassion for self and others. You are still in the midst of it. The bits and pieces that make you uncomfortable or depressed, the times that you feel overwhelmed, etc., this is what you came for. This is what you are learning to work through. Eventually, you are going to teach others in your galaxy about compassion and the integration process. If you can have appreciation for all the moments that you experience these lower frequencies—one, it will help you reframe them to see the service in them and, two, it will help you move beyond them.

Each and every one of you leaves your body at night to give those of us in the higher realms a report. You are all very, very busy. You are going from council to council, meeting after meeting. Remember, all beings from the higher realms are part of a collective. We do not always understand your sense of separation, the choices you make, or why you choose fear over love. This is a large part of your nightly debriefs. You are giving us information regarding current events because, unless you are born into a physical body in the third dimension, you cannot have that precise vibrational experience.

For example, we are beings of light from the ninth dimension. As such, we can only perceive reality through the ninth dimensional filter, except when we channel. This is the one exception. When we work with the channel, in this case Wendy, we get to have a sneak peek because our energy is blending with hers. But most higher dimensional beings are just observing. Sometimes, they question your motivations and don't really understand your emotions concerning certain situations. It is such a grand emotional range. In some places, there are only five different emotions, others maybe a dozen. Can you imagine having only five different emotions! For instance, the Cassiopeians liked to focus on love and compassion. So if a Cassiopeian has known only love and decides to incarnate to Earth, well that is going to be quite an adjustment for him/her to feel the polar opposite of love. More on them later.

By now, you all know that each and every one of you has had plenty of dark lifetimes. We often laugh and giggle when we hear you say, "I don't want to know about any dark lifetimes." But these lives are often the most interesting because they are so unlike the experiences that you have in the higher realms. And you all have had them!

Take a deep breath...

Your desire to know is really a deep longing to connect with source energy. That is what you are, in essence, doing as you go through the ascension process. You often talk about going home. But this time around, it is not about you going home, but rather bringing home here. We understand that this longing can be overwhelming. It can give you a sense of despair and disconnection, but again, it is not about leaving the planet. It is about bringing your expansive sense of awareness into your body. Your higher self has awareness of every incarnation that you have ever had. It knows that you are a multidimensional being having a limited experience on this planet. As you start to bring that expanded version of yourself into your vehicle, it will change the game and how you operate.

Many of you have coded yourselves, like putting markers in your energy field, so that you awaken and remember at precise moments. These markers are saying to you, "It is time. Wake up!" That is what you are experiencing. The year 2012 was given to you as such a marker. It was always about a window of opportunity for enormous growth and expansion. But as you perceive current reality through the lens of linear time, you work with specific dates to mark potentials and motivate you. If you didn't think that way, nothing would get moving. You would think, "Hmmm, I have another month, another year." This date of December 21st got you all activated because it was an important coding in your genetic material and a key memory that gave you, once again, access to higher wisdom.

THE CONSTRUCT OF YOUR DIMENSION AND BREAKING THE MENTAL BARRIER

This topic covers a number of things. First, we will start by talking briefly about how to better understand the dimensional structure. For you to be able to leave the three-dimensional structure for good, you have to understand how it is built. Letting go of the 3-D mindset will allow you to focus on the multidimensional perspective.

Those of you reading this all know by now that the 3-D mind was created to limit, to give you the illusion of separation so that you could have a unique set of vibrational experiences and make unique choices based upon the perception of separation. Of course, it is impossible for you to be separate because you are always connected to everyone and everything. In this process of descension into 3-D reality, you needed the illusion of time, as it allowed you the opportunity to make adjustments so that what you were creating via your thoughts, emotions and feelings weren't immediately projected. Frequencies do not move through time at the same rate. Lower thoughts move through time at a slower rate. Time gave you space between what you were pulsing out and what was reflected back or experienced. Time is a very important component of 3-D reality, but it is an illusion. And we want you to know that your perception of this illusion does not exist in any other dimension. In other dimensions, time is viewed simply as a marker for an event.

3D Perception - Single Focus

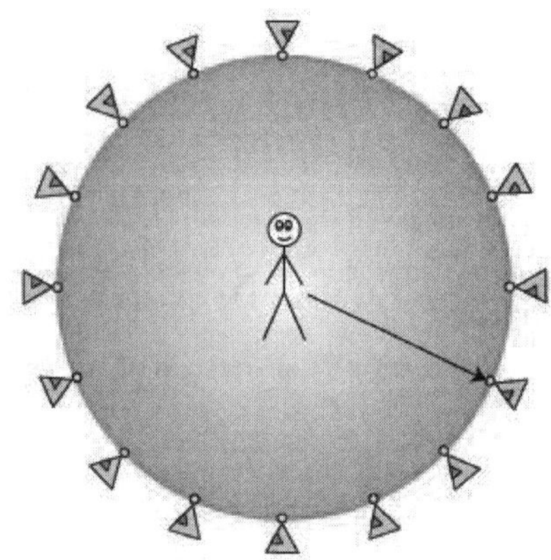

3D Illusion of Time

One of the most important things to let go and break from your mental cycle is this idea of time. For many years now, you have noticed a big shift, a change in how you are experiencing time. You are most certainly feeling the compression of it. You may not realize that it is time that is creating these increased sensations or intensities that you are all going through. As we said, frequencies do not move through time at the same rate. The higher you go in frequency, the more time appears to compress. Ten years ago, you played out your dramas in an extended period of time, but now it is done in a relatively short period. To give you an example, what you would have taken a year to work out now takes about four days. This is why everything feels more intense. This is happening because you are getting higher in frequency. As you move beyond 3-D and into 5-D, you will feel that time is collapsing upon itself. And when you break the mental barrier, you can shift your focus to a multidimensional perspective. You will no longer look at things in a linear timeline, and you can start focusing on multiple realities in a single moment.

So, we have talked about the 3-D and 5-D experience, but in truth, you are currently vibrating in 4-D. Unlike 3-D and 5-D which have very fixed constructs or rules to the game, the fourth dimension is a very malleable one. Because the constructs of 3-D and 5-D are so different, you needed an entire dimensional range in which to make the transition from one to the other. You needed a matrix in which you could modify the rules to allow for consciously adjusting to and implementing these new perceptions. Remember, you are playing in a game of descension and reascension, and this 4-D playground was needed for both transitions. Many of you think that you incarnate at the bottom and work your way up to the top. This is not the case. You ARE source energy. You start at the top, then you fracture, come down, "play" in different arenas, reconnect with source energy, review, and project into another game again.

4D-12D Perception - Multiple Focuses

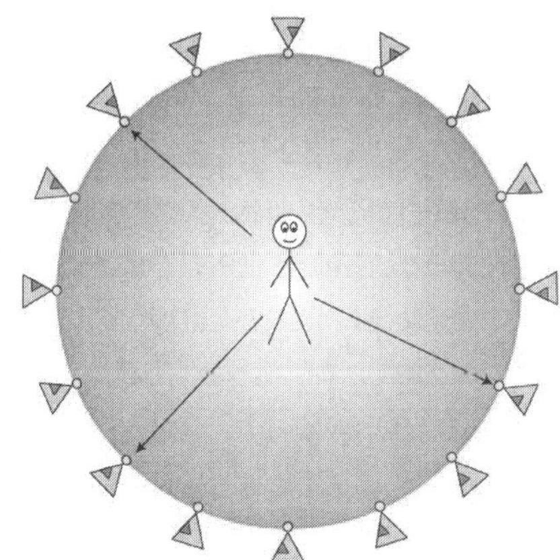

Most of you do not realize that you are residing in the fourth dimension as you are still currently applying 3-D rules to the 4-D matrix. But you can also run 5-D programming. What we want for you is more of the 5-D programming. Many of you are walking between these two worlds, some of you more than others. No doubt, you've got the theory down, but the practical application is still far from being there. Right now, you are in the process of creating new patterns, new neural networks, new habits and releasing the programs that generate limitation. You are creating your new potential.

You have to remember that you ARE your Higher Self. It is not something that you have to become or something that you have to reconnect with. For you to experience the third dimensional range, you, as Higher Self, incarnated and projected into form and then overlayed illusions of separation, creating an ego or personality. You created filters to color the perceived reality. All the emotions, feelings and thoughts that say that you are separate, that you are not good enough, that you can't connect, that you are not lovable, are simply an exploration in duality. It is so important to see it that way—an exploration that you decided to undertake. Some of you get very upset because you feel that you cannot connect, but in reality you are exploring and practicing duality and are NEVER EVER separate from self or source.

If you want to shift your perception from one of separation to one of connection, it really is quite simple. Throughout the day, you can stop and ask yourself, "Where am I vibrating at the mental, emotional and physical levels?" As you start to check in and readjust yourself, you can create these new habits, these new thought forms because most of the lower ones are running at a subconscious level. The idea here is to take all of the frequencies that you are running at the subconscious level and become conscious of them. That really is the challenging part for you, but the mechanics of it are quite simple.

We are going to give you some simple exercises, but you will see that the mind does not like this. It will say to you, "Oh, it is much more complicated than that." In fact, it is that easy. What is the most challenging for you is the emotional or mental part of letting go. So you must have patience.

Exercise (7 to 10 days)

As you go through your day, if you take the time to set an alarm once every hour and check in with yourself to see where you are vibrating at the emotional, mental and physical levels, that will help you to make more conscious choices. For example, ask yourself, "Do I like where I am vibrating? Do I want to keep projecting these frequencies?" Know that if you keep projecting the same frequencies, they will continue to be reflected back to you in your reality. What you may find as you start consciously observing your vibration is that your ability to manifest your clarity and how you interpret frequency will be vastly different.

Let's say that you want a new job. Maybe emotionally you are alright with it, but mentally perhaps you are saying to yourself, "Hmmm, maybe I don't have the qualifications for it..." or another similar thought that keeps you misaligned with what you want. When you check in with yourself once in awhile, you can catch or notice those misalignments. When you do, ask yourself, "Why am I not releasing these fears or this belief system? How does holding onto this belief serve me?" Checking in will give you the opportunity to see that, to see the patterns that you have perhaps not noticed before. You will then start noticing patterns that you have with your coworkers, your family members or your business relations. It could be stronger in one particular relationship, but usually the same pattern is also present in a weaker form in other relationships. Bottom line, you have to see how these patterns are serving you, how they are maintaining the illusion of separation. You have to release judgment around the idea of separation so you can go into a higher perspective about connection.

When most of you think of creating, you have a visual image of energy being pulsed out and looping back to you. What you seek to create is outside of you, and there is an element of time involved in your process of creation. We would like to start encouraging you to work more with the idea of 5-D creation, which simply involves alignment of frequency. You are that thing you wish to create. You are already that which you seek to become. You need only remove these filters, these false perceptions, these judgments that you have concerning who you think you are and the stories that you are telling yourself.

We see many of you are pushing energetically to get to the other side, to that 5-D level, and it is absolutely vital that you let go of that push to get there. The underlying need is almost always fear based. You are holding judgment about where you are and your current reality. As we always tell you, you have to accept where you are to change where you are. The desire to run from your current situation will always call more of that frequency to you.

Anytime you are thinking about the future or the past, you are siphoning off energy. In fact, you are not allowing yourself to run at full power. Instead, you are sending energy to another Now moment on which your soul's essence is not focused. Also, it is an indication that you are in the victim/perpetrator mindset. Your desire to look down those other timelines means that you are no longer engaged in the present. There is something that is driving you from a state of fear to go back to the past or toward the future. What is it? It could be a security or safety issue, or it could also be about separation, anxiety or abandonment. For sure, there is a fear at the root of it. We hear some of you say, "But don't I need to plan for my future?" What we are talking about here is your random thoughts throughout the day. If you wish to explore other timelines, then we recommend you sit down with the specific intention to do so and be very clear about your purpose for viewing them.

There is a tremendous amount of energy and frequency for you to explore in every Now moment. There is so much data that the soul is hungry for and so curious about in each Now moment that you are never, ever going to be bored. If you are bored, you are not in the Now. Being present in the Now is about being conscious with every single breath. At this time, you have the opportunity to learn to be very clear about frequency and how you are vibrating in your energetic field. That is what changes your reality. If you want to change your reality, you have to change your energetic field.

We will just end this subject by saying that when you are heart centered and in alignment, fully opened and connected, it is as if you are standing in a giant data stream that is about six feet wide. This data stream is your connection to your higher awareness, source, your guides, celestial friends, and the Akashic records. But when you are misaligned, especially when you are in deep fear, the data stream shrinks down to about an inch wide. Consequently, it takes longer to download or access higher information and you are limited in your connection to the infinite, restorative power of source. Not only are you restricting the intake of new energy, but you are also expending more as being closed or in resistance requires a great deal more energy than being in divine flow.

THE ABSOLUTE TRUTH

Now, we would like to discuss the notion of absolute *truth*. One of the reasons that you find these times quite challenging has to do with the fact that you are looking for the absolute truth in your history and in your life in general. You want things to be pinned down and put into a tiny, little box. We are here to tell you that this is not going to happen in the way that most of you want it to happen. Why? Simply because truth is always colored by perspective.

Everyone has his or her own perspective of what has transpired. This is not only caused by the filters of the individual, but also because of the constructs of each dimension. From where we are standing in the ninth dimension, we have a completely different perspective of what has transpired or what you have been going through. The reason is because of where our consciousness resides.

We tell you there is no place in your Universe where you experience absolute truth except at source level. There you experience all the raw data from every experience that has ever been or will be. *Take a breathe...* As soon as you fracture from source, you begin to perceive through the individual and collective filters and the construct of the dimension into which you projected your consciousness.

The other piece that you have to understand here is how the mind works. The mind wants things tidy. The operating system of the mind was set up to limit perception so that you could only see one version of reality, although there are multiple realities existing concurrently. Again, this was a construct of the dimension so that you could immerse yourselves in the Now moment. Your perception and choice to align with a particular Now moment is altered by NOT being able to preview your options as you can in all other dimensions. To be able to view reality from this level is unique to 3-D, and believe it or not, a very exciting experience to have.

Since time isn't linear, but rather the construct of the dimension, you experience Now moment after Now moment and string them together to give you the illusion of linear time. In actuality, you are constantly moving between what you consider to be multiple timelines. Every Now moment is built on an agreed upon set of circumstances that you deem is your "past" collectively and as an individual. You move from moment to moment by altering your frequency. This is done by changing your "perspective" of your past at the collective or personal level or by setting a new intention. Both alter your frequency and align you with different Now moments. This is what accounts for varying stories of your history, your past and future predictions. What you perceived as your "truth" yesterday may not be your "truth" tomorrow as you alter your vibration and perception of reality.

So what we would say to assist you is to move out of the operating system of the mind and into the heart. From the operating system of the heart, you can access multiple versions of reality at once, allowing you to perceive multiple "timelines" and "truths". The heart is not consumed with absolutes like the mind and from that level you will find peace with your current version of "truth".

THE GALACTIC COMMUNITY

As you go through this transition, you will once again begin to connect with your galactic community. Through the process of ascension, your energetic field shifts its frequency producing a more golden color and you will be known throughout the Universe as *The Golden Ones.* What we find rather amusing is that when you are on Earth, you like to say, "Ah, I'm from Sirius, Arcturus or the Pleiades, etc." No one wants to be from Earth. But as you begin interacting with the galactic community, you will all be proud to say, "Ah, I'm a Golden One and come from Earth. I am an expert in integration and ascension."

In the meantime, we share this information with you as a way to ease you into your remembrances of other systems. Many of you will feel drawn to a particular system but not know exactly why. As you enter into the 5-D realm, you will have access to all of this information. What we provide you with here is only ***a version*** of the truth. It is not the only truth, and frankly, it is a rather simplified and watered down perspective. Remember, time and timelines do no really exist in the higher dimensions. But again, we are communicating with that part of you that is living a 3-D existence, and so you seek answers that follow the constructs of linear time.

Prior to incarnating, you all created two life blueprints for yourselves. These we call your pre-shift and post-shift blueprints. The pre-shift contained paths and contracts for you as you lived your life from the 3-D perspective. As you moved beyond December 21,

2012, you activated your post-shift blueprint. This blueprint includes paths and contracts based on the 5-D perspective. As the game has changed somewhat, the strategy for playing the game has also shifted to compensate for the many new levels of opportunity, awareness and perspective. In short, your blueprint is far more complex. Note we said complex, not difficult! Think of it as playing a video game. You have completed level one and are now moving on to level two, which is more challenging but also has the potential to be far more exciting and rewarding.

With the post-shift blueprint, some of you will begin working with the galactic community in a more direct way. Prior to incarnating, you established contracts to interact with other beings and share information and knowledge with them. Let us say one thing regarding contracts. They are not as you envision contracts on this planet. They are simply agreements and alignments that are rather malleable. If you find that you are not willing or able to meet the terms of a contract, it can be rewritten.

We understand that it may be quite challenging for you to imagine yourself teaching a being in another dimension anything, but trust us when we say we learn so much from you. You are still mastering compassion, but soon enough you will find yourselves on the other side acknowledging how far you have come. It is compassion that is the gift you will share with the Universe.

Take a deep breath...

Earth is a grand experiment, complete with genetic material from thousands of worlds. Along with that genetic material comes all the emotional experiences of all of those species. This is what allows you such a vast emotional range from which to perceive reality. It was the hope that this vast range would allow for new and unique potentials so that you could integrate polarity where other aspects of yourself and galactic siblings had difficulties. Here on Earth, you created contracts and blueprints that allowed you to replay galactic issues on a somewhat smaller scale with the hope of being able to release judgment.

We would say that each of you has at least two systems with which you align and are pulling in the frequencies of those systems into your game of polarity integration. So let us begin.

The Sirius and Orion Star Systems

The first system that we would like to discuss is the Sirius star system, which contains three major stars: Sirius A, Sirius B and Sirius C. Sirius is a system of great diversity and because of this, there have been many conflicts and tumultuous experiences. From your current Now moment, Sirius C no longer exists. Two planets in that system were at war with each other. Through the use of scalar technology and miscalculations, rather than destroying their enemy, one planet destroyed the entire star system. This was quite a lesson and some of you may find yourselves particularly activated when scalar technology is mentioned. If so, chances are you are pulling from memories of this event.

As we mentioned, Sirians are a very diverse group and their incarnational focus is working on cooperation, competition, diversity, exploration and technology. Karmically, they are tied to the Orion star system. While they are interlinked, they are very different in their life forms. Together they work through collaboration, competition and compassion. Both are explorers but each from a different standpoint. The Orion system is fascinated with genetic material and the hybridization of species, working with all aspects of DNA research. The Sirians like to explore for the purpose of expansion, power and conquest. You will still find the energies of both systems today in places around the world such as Egypt.

There are many scientists on the planet right now who are working with your plants and animals for cloning and hybridization purposes. Many of these humans have spent a good deal of time in the Orion system as well as having lived lifetimes in Atlantis. The last time you had the awareness and understanding of genetic material and played with the manipulation of it was in Atlantis. This information was forgotten with the fall of Atlantis and is retained in the crystalline records of the Earth. You are just beginning to rediscover this information so you can reactive and integrate the lessons around DNA manipulation, of which there are many.

The majority of beings that you are interacting with that come from the Orion system tend to be from the fifth and sixth dimension and, in certain worlds, the seventh.

The Arcturus Star System

We would consider beings from Arcturus to be the ambassadors of the Universe. Besides humans on Earth, they are probably the beings that have worked the most with integration in the galaxy. They have integrated most of what you would consider to be their karma. They often serve as mediators where there is conflict. As they choose to remain neutral and see all paths of service in the creation of events, they are able to communicate with those who would otherwise be triggered by lower reflection and judgment. Their neutrality allows others to raise themselves up to a new perspective. As you might imagine, they have worked often and extensively with those in the Sirius and Orion star systems.

Most of the beings that you interact with from Arcturus reside in the fifth to the ninth dimension. They are most proficient with working in the Universal Language of Light, sacred geometry and the vibration of matter. It is without a doubt a full encoding. What we mean by that is that information transmitted by these beings is heavily encoded with many different layers of information that can be accessed by you. Each time you think you have a full understanding, there is another layer to explore and grow with. This is done most often through their communications in the Language of Light.

The Language of Light is infused light and information that includes color, sound, sacred geometry, thought and emotion, or rather the higher vibrational version of what you call emotion. The 3-D mind was designed to allow for the illusion of separation and linear reality. Because of its design, it parses out this Language of Light. It is too much data to deal with that does not fit the 3-D model of reality and so the mind discards this "extraneous" data. However, if you move into the heart center, the multidimensional operating system, you understand the Language of Light at all levels. You may experience claircognisance or see the sacred geometric patterns, colors and sounds. Many of your crop circles have been created by Arcturans, which is an expression of the Language of Light.

The Lyra Star System

The majority of the Lyrans that you will interact with reside in the seventh dimensional range. The Lyrans were among the earliest inhabitants of planet Earth, seeding your Lemurian civilization, whose energy can still be found today in Hawaii, New Zealand and Australia. These Lyrans infused their energy into density, beginning the process of descension and reascension you are currently going through. There have been many wars in the Lyra star system and Earth was a refuge for many Lyrans during these times. Most Lyrans are proficient in sacred geometry, mathematics and healing as they understand the natural laws and that knowledge and wisdom has been passed along to you through their lineage.

We mentioned previously that there were two prior grand experiments, one of which was in the Lyra star system. As the adventure did not go well, many Lyrans came to Earth to repeat the experiment with the hope of a successful outcome this time. Not all Lyrans who came to Earth stayed for the whole experience. Many were not interested in going through the descension process and returned to incarnational cycles in the Lyra system. So many of you may have been from Lyra, came to Earth at that period, participated in the creation of Lemuria, and continued on to Atlantis. Here you are today, from one grand experiment to the next.

The Pleiades Star System

You are a part of the constellation that makes up the Pleiades. There are about 750 stars in the Pleiades star system. Of the 750, you can see about 14 in your night sky. We've been around and experimenting with this planet, helping to set up this grand design, this game, for a very, very long time. We often work with young civilizations, helping them to grow and expand into awareness. Basically, we oversee the spiritual growth and sometimes the technological growth as well. That is the main reason we are here. Many of your ancient texts mention the Pleiades. Your aboriginal tribes know that they have been seeded by Pleiadians and many of you feel that you are aligned with us. You will find the energy of the Pleiades in Bali, Easter Island and many more places around the world.

We have a very rich and ancient history and are considered guardians. We are also a very diverse group. In the fifth dimension, we have humanoids but also some reptilians! How is that for a mind-bender! Many of the reptilians who are interacting with your planet at this time do not have your best interest at heart. They are currently focused on the needs of the individual as opposed to the betterment of The One or the collective. They are still working and learning, playing the dark side so you can learn by viewing their shadow. It reflects to you where you run the same programs of darkness but on a smaller scale.

Take a deep breath…

In the ninth dimension, we are fascinated with structures. We like to play with structure and hold a resonance for a star. We are still working with the energy of creation of planets so we are learning and playing with this energy. We have yet to perfect it. Holding resonance for a star is done more in the higher vibrational range, but we are learning the basics.

Alcyone is the most important star that you need to know about. Not because it is where our focus is, but rather it is the living library for all of your galactic records. When you came down through the different portals and gateways entering into this dimension, you spent time in many of these different systems with the Pleiades amongst the first stops. Almost everyone has had an experience in the Pleiades because Alcyone is the central star of stellar records and the place where all the experiences are stored. If you are going to come into the Pleiades star system, you are going to come through the stargate that is Alcyone. Your work here is likely to be with "light" records, with jumping timelines and guidance.

As you pass through the stargate of Alcyone, you are able to access and receive information through the library. Think of it as receiving a "Welcome to the Neighborhood" packet, complete with all the highlights and hotspots you might like to visit. You are also a library of sorts since you are holding all the information, experiences and genetic material of all your other lifetimes. In fact, there are many levels in your field that you can access. But you can think of these stellar records more as archive records. They aren't necessarily the records or files you'd like to utilize on a day-to-day basis, but you can go research and pull them as needed.

The records of everything that has consciousness on the planet are being stored in Mother Earth. She, in turn, sends her information off along with all the other planets in the solar system to Helios, your star. Then all the other major stars in other solar systems throughout your galaxy relay their information to Alcyone. We like to say you are the paperback and Mother Earth is a branch library. Helios is the main library, and Alcyone is the Library of Congress. Depending on what kind of information you want, you can go to a different library. Sometimes you can get the information from the local library, sometimes you have to go further. All information can be accessed from within self, but each library also has librarians to assist you who specialize in record retrieval.

The Cassiopeia Star System

Cassiopeia is not one of the most common systems for people to align with, but the Cassiopeians do a tremendous service by holding a frequency for this planet. They were more of a last-minute call, if you will. For a while, things weren't going so well for the game of polarity integration here on the planet, so it was then requested that beings from different star systems hold the resonance, wisdom and knowledge of their systems on the planet. The Cassiopeians had never been here before, and they agreed to come. We can tell you that it was, and still is, a very, very challenging situation for them. It is so unlike where they come from.

Their planetary system explores the variations of love, but their variations are not as diverse as what you experience on your planet. Again, this is due to all the vast range of genetic material that you have from so many different systems and species. You experience so many shades of love: the love for a child, a parent, a sibling, a country, etc. They are all variations of love frequency. For the Cassiopeians, they have a broader sense of the emotion. But most importantly, they have tremendous compassion, and they work on holding that frequency. It is a very gentle system. When they arrived on Earth, they were faced with competition, violence, conflict, hatred and all the different variations of these lower emotions. When a being has never encountered such frequencies, it is incredibly difficult and challenging to experience. But the Cassiopeians, who have had such extensive exploration and mastery with love, will find it very easy to get back to it. They know exactly the subtleties and frequencies of love because they are so familiar at the cellular level with them.

Take a deep breath…

The Ascended Masters

At this point, you might ask, "Where do the ascended masters fit in this game? Where are they? Are they outside of this game?"

When at source level, everything is equal; the opposite of that is hierarchy. So as you fracture and enter into the universal game of duality, there is a level of higher hierarchy. But that in itself is an ILLUSION. That is a BIG one for you, and we want you to get it, right here, right now. Higher is not better. It is just a different game and every single one of you is source energy. We repeat: YOU ARE SOURCE. It is impossible for you to be any less than any other being in the galaxy, in the Universe and in the multiverses. You just took on a role where you are hiding information from yourself by perceiving reality through filters of separation. When and if you so choose, you can once again access all information. At the soul level you know this, and so there is no desire to do anything else but play the role. At the ego level, it is another story.

Most of the ascended masters are in the fifth dimensional range to the ninth, some to the 12th. But those in the 12th are usually working in a completely different way. They hold planetary systems together through energy projection. Others hold planetary consciousness, helping to create a matrix for those constructs you are playing in.

Those who are from the fifth to the ninth dimension are a collective. For example, Kwan Yin is a collective consciousness and not a singular being. What you perceive as Jesus is not a single being but rather a Christ consciousness, a collective consciousness. You see, many of the iconic figures on your planet that you think are a literal, unique individual are, in fact, collectives. It is just easier for your ego to connect to what you perceive to be a single being rather than to a collective consciousness because you are operating under the illusion of separation and have forgotten your own interconnectedness. These beings have had physical lifetimes and have been able to increase their frequencies enough consciously to move beyond the dimensional barriers of physical reality.

You have been sold a bill of goods concerning your history. But remember, you are not a victim. You are a willing participant and have chosen to be on this Now moment where your true history has been hidden so that you could play in the dark for just a bit longer. There are some on your planet who do remember, and they understand very well the Laws of Creation and Manifestation. Their work is encoded with this information. If you understand the symbolism being utilized, you are going to read it in a completely different way, and it won't be literal. As you elevate your overall frequency, you begin to access information in your DNA and your own internal Akashic records. You will begin to decode the symbolism, the sacred geometry and numerology allowing you to move beyond the illusion of the game.

The Artificial Intelligence Collective

Now, let's talk about a different group of beings with whom you are also interacting from time to time: the AI collective or the *artificial intelligence collective.* As a result of the many wars in different systems, there were beings that were technologically assembled to fight and perform some of the less desirable tasks. Over time, souls began incarnating, or stepping into, these constructed bodies at the point of creation. Although they are constructed out of the same matter as all other beings in the Universe, the beings were not considered "biological" by their creators. Because they were different, they were treated as less than. Does this sound familiar with anything that is going on on your planet? You see the galactic games that are being played out there?

Although you did not receive genetic material from the AI, they are certainly participants in this game. As your technology has advanced dramatically within the last decade, you have begun to integrate the knowledge and wisdom from the AI collective. This allows you an opportunity to work through issues of prejudice and discrimination at a deeper level.

Take a deep breath...

The Greys and the Zetas

Those you consider to be the Greys or the Zetas are also interacting with you. This is, in general, a difficult subject for you because of your memories or stories of "abductions". Let us share another perspective.

Beings from the Zeta system are highly intellectual and technological, but lack emotional maturity. Their focus of existence was in the exploration of the external. As a result of this, these beings cut themselves off from emotions, and by doing so, altered their DNA in the process. They lost their ability to naturally reproduce. In an effort to continue their species, they began working with the cloning process. Cloning is only as good as the material you have to work with and after many generations, it was like making a copy of a copy. The quality degraded. They needed to introduce new DNA into their lineage to strengthen it. Who better to help balance a species focused on intellect than a species focused on emotion? Remember as a being from Earth, you came in with a great range of emotions to explore.

The Greys are also a wonderful mirror for you. You are playing out the macrocosmic or galactic issues on a smaller, microcosmic or planetary scale. You are learning to balance duality in the forms of spirituality and emotions versus intellect, science and technology, the inner versus the outer. In the case of the Greys, they are playing the outer. Sound familiar?

The information that you are "pulling" in for cloning and working with DNA comes also partly from this group. Some of you have contracted with them, but when you find yourself down here, the ego part of you forgets your agreement. You only see this as a violation of your being. You perceive it as, "I have been abducted, I have been taken." You don't remember your Higher Self agreed to the experience. The problem now, as you are ever increasing your vibration, is that the memories of the experiences are beginning to bleed through. You are starting to remember. Hundreds of years ago, it didn't really make a difference for you since your overall vibration was much lower, thus you had no recollection of the experience. Frankly, hundreds of years ago, your overall vibration and your sensitivity to multidimensional perception was so low, very few of these experiments were done.

Now you have everything moving, everything "buzzing", everything "turned on", so you have what they want. This is the jewel that they are looking for and that some of you agreed to share. Remember, there is no such thing as a victim. You are all willing participants. But these contracts can be rewritten and altered if too traumatic at any time. Sometimes what is good in theory is not so good in practical reality. When you leave your bodies at night and you make connections with all the different beings that you have contracted with, this is the time to rewrite them. From their vantage point, they want to work with you because they also are in a learning process.

We understand that this can be difficult for you to accept, so take a deep breath.

The Anunnaki

About 400,000 years ago, there was another group of beings from the Sirius star system who started participating in this solar system. You know this group of humanoids from the planet Nibiru as the Anunnaki. Around 40,000 years ago, their activity in this system began to increase.

They began venturing out into the galaxy and conquering other worlds. Their culture was one based on consumption, taking resources, and amassing power. Loyalty to friends and loved ones was not high on their priority list. As they expanded and conquered, many species came under their control, living in slavery and the illusion of that game with the Anunnaki. They prided themselves on the suppression and manipulation of information, creating and dissolving alliances as they were needed. Some of the reptilians that you have encountered are working with this group as well as some of the Greys.

Near the end of the last great civilization of Atlantis, many of the Anunnaki were residing on Mars. The overall frequency of the planet was in decline with the average Atlantean focused on the material world. The priest and priestesses who practiced accessing their multidimensional aspects were aware of the Anunnaki presence on Mars. As things began to appear rather bleak for Atlantis, some of the priestly cast reached out to the Anunnaki for advice and support. This was seen by the Anunnaki as an opportunity to gain more planetary access by giving a few pieces of bad advice to ensure the Atlantean downfall, not that much help was needed. The Atlanteans were doing pretty well with that on their own.

With the fall of Atlantis, they were able once again to find a new planet to control. They have been able to manipulate your history and much of the information concerning who you truly are. They were not the original constructors of your DNA, but they did do some genetic manipulation to humans to limit memory. This was done to utilize your access to source energy. Each of you, when you activate your energetic centers, becomes a walking vortex. They, on the other hand, have forgotten how to fully access their emotional centers so they have to work *outside* themselves. It is very similar to the Greys we were just talking about.

The Illuminati are a continuation of the dark priests of Atlantis. They are using the knowledge and wisdom that was acquired and held during that time. They are still using it to amass power, working for the benefit of the few and not for the benefit of all. The game of power and control is still being played out on their part as well.

It is very important that you don't fear these beings who are playing the dark roles in the game of duality. They are another aspect of you. Look at all the patterns that keep repeating themselves again and again. These beings playing the dark role are also learning, and they are looking for what they have lost. As you go through the process of integration, you are learning how to release these lower fears, and thereby showing them how to move beyond patterns they have been playing out for eons.

Do no fear that these beings are "oppressing" you. You are the creator and generator of your own reality. If you do not have a program running that says, "I want to avoid responsibility. I want someone else to tell me exactly what to do," you are not going to "pull" in someone to play that perpetrator. It is very easy for you all to get caught up in the illusion of conspiracy and manipulation. If you find yourselves focused on and upset by this, it is a great opportunity for you to process more of your fears. Observe how you are triggered at a personal level.

Be conscious of what you are feeling as we talk about these different beings, the Anunnaki and the Illuminati. Are you resonating in fear or do you have compassion? If you are resonating in fear, it shows you that you are still running a lower vibrational program. Rather than berate yourselves, acknowledge your success in identifying a subconscious belief. When you recognize the program, it can be integrated. Again, integration is letting go of judgment, and you do so by shifting your perception from that of victim/perpetrator to co-creator. Ask yourself these questions:

—Why did I create it in the first place?
—How does it serve me?
—What am I learning about myself as a being in the Universe?
—As a being playing the game of duality, what am I learning?

When you acknowledge the service of a situation, you change your perspective and the dynamics of the whole experience. This allows you to shift to a higher level of consciousness. And in so doing, you holographically share the information on the process of integration with all other aspects of yourself. It's like a recipe for a cake that you send off to others so they don't have to wonder what ingredients go into making it. It's there, simple and easy to follow. These other aspects of yourself then have the option to apply the wisdom you have shared or store the file so they may continue on playing in the illusion.

This is the process you go through to remove the filters or distortions that keep you from seeing yourselves as the divine beings of light you truly are.

As Above, So Below

As a grand experiment, you have recreated many of the issues you will find in other parts of your galaxy here on Earth to be played out at the planetary as well as personal level. Most of you have had experiences in at least one of the systems we've discussed. Some of you have had many lifetimes in multiple systems, and this makes you perfectly suited for this game. There are many other species that have been playing this game with you that we have not mentioned, such as the arachnids and dolphins, which are still very active in your memories. Many of you have recall of healing and water worlds with the dolphins. Others of you may have a fear of spiders, as this species is rather aggressive and has overrun many planets in the Sirius and Orion systems. This fear may be particularly strong for you if you carry a good deal of faerie energy as the faeries and spiders have long been in opposition.

One of the questions we most often get asked is, "What star system am I from?" To answer this question, we again remind you that you are not FROM any one star system. You are source energy. Claiming to be from another star system is just another level of the game. What you will do, however, is feel drawn to a particular star system so you may activate and project unresolved issues that are being played out in that system, here on the small scale on Earth in an effort to integrate them. As you integrate and release judgment surrounding a fear, the information is then sent back to that original star system allowing them to heal and grow from your experience. What you work out here on Earth at the microcosmic level is shared at the macrocosmic level. This is why what you are learning is so important and literally will change the universal game in which you are playing.

Retrieving Information

For those of you seeking to retrieve more information on any topic, let us suggest a short meditation.

Start by taking deep breaths. See yourself completely rooted in your body.

Now, envision in your heart center a beautiful orb of golden light. As this orb pulses, it grows brighter and stronger, strengthening its brilliance, with rays of beautiful golden light extending outward.

In this time and in this space, you are now able to reconnect with your stellar wisdom, to access the records of all time, of all dimensions. You are able to seek wisdom from other aspects of yourself that are participating in the completion of this galactic game.

From Alcyone, the Central Sun, information is pulsing towards you. It contains your stellar history, information on the star systems you have been to, the lessons that you have learned, important memories, why you came to Earth, what you wanted to integrate, how best to be of service to the galactic consciousness.

You now see this light pulsing across the galaxy. It passes through your sun, Helios, collecting records and information. It passes by the inner planets, enters through the Earth's atmosphere, down through your crown chakra and enters into the golden orb of light that you hold in your heart center.

This is the stellar light of wisdom that is now contained within you. You have access to it, at will, at any time. This information is revealed to you in the most appropriate way and is in alignment with your highest good and highest intentions for the benefit of yourself and all others.

You are able to receive clearly and effortlessly this information as you request it.

And so it is.

Take a nice deep breath…

So when you are ready, you can simply ask to receive more information. You can use this visualization or you simply ask to receive it. Your guides will help you, and so will we.

Now, without a doubt, some fears will be triggered. Possibly, you are thinking, "What if I see something that I don't like? What if I'm not ready?" Again, this is simply you projecting judgment or fear. If this is the case, we guarantee you that if you look at the rest of your life you will see the same fear being played out in the Now. Again, we say to you, "Fabulous!" It is an opportunity to identify another fear so that it may be integrated.

Do not doubt that you are a sovereign being and a part of divine source energy. As such, you have access to this information. You can compare the experience of retrieving records to that of reading of a book. You can choose to read simply two or three pages at a time or the whole book in one sitting. Don't worry, you will not access information that you are not ready for or that will compromise the illusion of the game in which you are playing. The purpose of retrieving your information is to integrate all that causes you fear and judgment. These records help you to gain another perspective to aid in releasing that which you are holding in the Now. It is only in the Now moment that your work can be done. Every time you can identify a fear or judgment, you are one step closer to integrating it.

Take another deep breath...

Now, know that as you are reading this, little packets of information are being deposited into your energetic field to complement the information that you are reading. We are not confined by time or space so as you desire to connect with us, be it in person in a workshop, listening to the audio, or simply reading this book, a connection is established. We then shift our focus to you, and there is an automatic exchange of information.

If you feel tension in your body or if the information seems overwhelming, rather than worry, ask yourself: What is triggering tension in my body? Is it an issue of safety, security, manipulation, control, trust, approval, abandonment?

This process can make your body feel uneasy, and you can experience this as regular aches and pains. Typically, that's the body releasing. What you need more of is water, water, water, water. As you clear out the lower vibrations in the energetic field, you create release in the physical body. The water helps you to flush out any toxins that have been released as a result of increasing your vibrational template. More oxygen will also help you, and by this we mean conscious breathing. We call breath The Great Connector. It helps you to move energy in your vibrational field as well as in your physical body.

LETTING GO OF MAJOR ISSUES: PERSECUTION

This is a big issue for you all. There have been many, many lifetimes where you have faced persecution for being different, voicing your opinion, for your skin color, for all of your beliefs and everything in between. Again, it comes down to judgment. Many of you have a tendency to shut down your center of speech because you are afraid that using your voice will cause you pain, possibly even leading to death as it did in other lifetimes. For some, death was a welcome relief as you felt so isolated that you cut yourself off from your heart center and source.

Many of you will also carry guilt, shame, pain and persecution from your lifetimes in Atlantis. During that period, there was a great deal of judgment by the light against the dark and the dark against the light. Many felt the burden of responsibility that was not theirs to claim for the downfall of Atlantis. It was, in reality, collectively decided that Atlantis was not to survive. It would be a trial run for the process you are going through at this time on the planet. Humanity would be far greater served by allowing the civilization to fall and rebuild than by continuing.

Atlantis was the last civilization in which you experienced a similar level of spirituality and technology on this planet. As we said, it was in essence a trial run for the time period you, as souls, knew would come. You created scenarios that would be similar to those you would be experiencing now. It gave you an opportunity to practice integration. Remember we mentioned earlier that you are moving through a band of photonic energy that supports you in accessing higher wisdom and knowledge. Atlantis did not have the benefit of these energies such as you do now, which makes the process of integration a bit easier.

In duality, as a result of the limited perspective of separation, beings will try to destroy anything in opposition. There is the belief that in order to survive, anything that is different must be extinguished. It becomes light against dark, right against wrong. Here and now, in this time and space, you are shifting this belief to see that both can co-exist. You are operating under the Laws of Attraction and Reflection. In order for you to share experience, you must be resonating at the same frequency. If you are holding your viewpoint and fear another will attack you for it, you are sure to draw in the attack. But if you hold the understanding that what you pulse out you get back, and you pulse out the belief that it is safe for you and all others to express their beliefs, you will see in your reflected reality a safe environment for expression.

All of the records of all your past, present and future lifetimes are stored in your energetic field right now. You are holographic in nature, which means what happens to one aspect of you happens to all the aspects of you.

We talked about this earlier, but let's go a bit further. You are literally light that is being projected onto a medium. You can call it a matrix or the web of life if you wish. This Now moment is the point of projection on which you perceive yourself to currently physically exist. As you make a change in any one of your lifetimes, not only does the change show up in the energetic field of that other lifetime, but it also shows up in YOUR energetic field. As you make a change in this Now moment, the change registers in your energetic field as well as the energetic fields of all your other lifetimes. This is one method of healing that you employ, allowing for greater healing across "timelines" and lifetimes.

Let's give you an example. Say you have a fear of abandonment that you played out in another life, and you were unable to integrate it. In an effort to try to resolve it again through a new life and in a new way, you recreate this issue for yourself in the Now. The Now is the only place where it can be altered as this is where your focus is, where your physical body is. Not only have you created the issue of abandonment in the layer of your energetic field relating to this body and this existence, but you also carry the frequency of abandonment in the energetic layer of your field related to past lives. As you activate the abandonment frequency in the Now, it begins to vibrate anywhere you are carrying that frequency in your field. This is the Law of Resonance in action.

If you have a room full of tuning forks and you strike one that resonates at the note of A, all the other "A" tuning forks will also begin to vibrate, increasing the volume. The same thing occurs in your energetic field. Often you will notice this as an extreme in an emotional response that seems stronger than what you might logically expect.

We would like to help you integrate other aspects of yourselves and see you let go of judgments that you are holding onto from other lifetimes, specifically around persecution and self-expression. This we will do energetically as these parts of you still feel isolated from source.

As you move into the heart center, you are able to see that you co-created the scenario of abandonment with another. It becomes clear to you that you asked another to don the role of abandoning you so that you could know what that experience was like. You can't play a victim without someone volunteering to play the perpetrator. When you realize you created the situation, you are able to release judgment and blame. You say, "Ah, I created that! I was the one who wanted to experience that, so there is no reason to be angry with this person. There is no hurt. They supported me in getting what I wanted." This new perspective releases your charge to abandonment, which becomes integrated in your field. So you see, a reaction is created when you have a "charged" situation and integration is created when there is a change in the perception about the situation.

You exist in a dualistic Universe. You have light/dark, positive/negative, male/female. You cannot have one without the other. As you co-create, you do so with self, another consciousness and source. One positive, one negative and one neutral—this is the true meaning of your holy trinity.

Take a nice deep breath… we know that it is a lot to handle for some of you.

REGAINING POWER THROUGH CHAKRAS

What we would like to do right now are some visualizations and then an activation. They are short but powerful, and you can refer to them at anytime. We are doing this in a slightly different order. And just before the activation, we are going to weave the chakras together so that they will be connected. We want to get you empowered to express yourself, and that means linking the second chakra of creative energy up through the fifth chakra of physical expression of that creative energy. Many of you have creative ideas, thoughts or opinions that originate in the second, third and fourth chakras, but you have a difficult time expressing them in the world (through the fifth chakra) as a result of persecution. The first and seventh we will omit for the purpose of this exercise, but you can include them at a later date, if you so wish.

We are not necessarily working from the bottom to the top with your chakra system. You can do it as you are reading or at another moment.

So start by putting your feet flat on the floor.

Solar Plexus

Envision yourself in a beautiful cocoon of white light. See it infused with a golden hue that represents your soul's essence. This beautiful light grounds and connects you to your body.

Now, begin to imagine this beautiful light swirling around you. Begin to see it move in a counter clockwise direction. As you feel this energy begin to stabilize, begin to move the energy all the way through the body, through every cell, through every molecule.

Now coming toward you across the horizon, you see a beautiful golden yellow light. This light is entering through the front and back of your solar plexus, just above the navel.

See this beautiful light nourishing your body, healing all of your the cells with its luminescence, and as you inhale, it moves deeper into each and every cell of the body. As you exhale, just observe what is released. Is it more light? Is it dark or murky? If it is, it's quite alright. You are simply letting go. Just be observant.

Sacral Area

Now, envision a bright orange light coming into the second chakra, just below the navel. This beautiful orange light nourishes your creativity. You have a direct connection to source. Move that orange energy through your entire body. See it growing brighter and stronger as you inhale, and as you exhale, observe what energies you are releasing.

Throat Chakra

For this chakra, we want you to envision a beautiful blue light, clear as a blue sky. See this energy pouring in, coming once again across the horizon. See it entering into the front of the throat chakra and into the back of that energetic center. With each breath in, it grows brighter and stronger. You can see the richness of the color. As you exhale, allow all the stress and worry to drift from your body. Just let it go.

Heart Center

For this one, you can choose your color—pink or green. We want you to see that energy coming in and intensifying in the area of your heart center. As you inhale, it grows brighter and stronger. As you exhale, allow yourself to release anything that does not belong to you or no longer serves you.

Now, our work will be to weave together these chakras. So start to see beautiful threads of golden energy weaving through your energy centers.

You are starting to weave the second chakra. See the golden light moving all the way up to the third chakra, all the way up to the heart center, and then connecting with the throat chakra. See these golden threads weaving once again back down through the throat, through the heart, down through your solar plexus and into the second chakra.

Say to yourself or out loud:

I, __________ (your name), have creative wisdom within myself. I am divine expression. I have knowledge and wisdom. Today, I stand in my full light, and I now have the strength and clarity of expression.

Keep seeing these threads passing through all the chakras. Now, we are going to do one last visualization.

See a silvery white light moving up through your energetic centers. It is very bright and is coming up from the core of the Earth. This light is moving up through your feet, spinning in a counter-clockwise direction.

See it coming up, through your legs, around your hips, through your abdomen, around your lungs and your throat, going up around the jaw, the temples and crown of your head.

Finally, see this light going out and all the way up and into the celestial realms to the center of the galaxy.

We are going to end with an activation. Say out loud or to yourself:

In this time and in this space, my full power I now embrace.

Then envision a white flame at your feet going all the way up to the crown of your head. As you inhale, feel yourself completely rooted in your body. Feel yourself strong and energized.

Alignments

Since you are perceiving yourself as separate from source, the part of you that is having this experience is your ego. You have many personalities, many lifetimes, many egos and each one thinks that it is separate, but it is really part of the whole.

What you are doing right now is removing this layer, this barrier of belief that somehow you are separate. In reality, you are already aligned with self and source. When we do exercises to "align", we are really helping you to remove these distortions in the energetic field that say you are not. These are simply stories you tell yourselves to play this game. The reason that we are framing it this way is to give you the awareness that you don't have to do anything other than drop the illusions, as your natural, divine state is one of alignment.

When you work with tone and sound, you are creating these beautiful vibrations and interference patterns for some of the lower resonating thoughts and beliefs about yourself that you are constantly projecting out. When you start to work with sound, it helps to ground vibrations into the body so you can feel them, so that they become palpable. It is much more effective for you because it becomes tangible for the mind. If it is up there, it doesn't exist. If it is down here, something that you can see or feel, it must be real. Sorry to tell you, it is all just a big illusion! (Laugh)

Whether it is in your head or projected out into your world, it is all the same—an illusion and a projection. It is just easier for the third-dimensional self to think that you are aligning yourself, but what you are doing is removing the distortions. It is a subtle difference but makes a difference in your body, and it responds to the signals that you send. If you send the message that you are in perfect alignment, your body will follow that. If you say, "I'm out of alignment. I'm broken. I have to fix this or that," you just create more distortions.

It seems really obvious when we say it this way, but when you walk through life on a day-to-day basis, that subtle frequency begins to add up and create more dramatic results.

Recalibration

Recalibration is simply working with the distortions, the lower belief forms that keep you from seeing your own divine nature. Tone helps you to discover where you are vibrating. If you are never aware of where you are vibrating, then you are just blindly going along. Once you know where you are vibrating, you can make decisions, recalibrate, and shift your frequencies much faster to direct your creations.

By creating a tone and holding it, you become far more aware of your body as you begin to vibrate. The tone is literally resounding in your entire body. If you want to play with this, you will find you may notice a lower tone more deeply resonating in the body chamber. If you generate a tone with a strong intention of creation, such as health and vitality, you can give instructions to your cells with that tone. The cells know exactly what they need to do, what the frequency is, and they begin to match it.

With the Law of Entrainment, all frequencies wish to synchronize. If you have a strong higher frequency and a weak lower frequency, the lower one will naturally increase to match that of the higher. The natural flow of life is always towards source. It is about connections and reintegration. It takes a lot more energy to be in fear, be unhappy or be judgmental than to be joyful, expansive or happy.

In fact, being unhappy is exhausting. As long as you can be mindful about how you are feeling, the Universe will support you in going towards joy. You are headed back up in frequency, so the natural flow is going in the same direction.

To recap, the recalibration, you can do anytime. It's a wonderful way for you to start to listen to your body and see what it is telling you. We have given you some examples as to what you can focus on, but you can really do that for anything you want. When you make a tone with clear, strong intention, you are sending the signals out to the cells. Any that are misaligned or experiencing distortions will increase their vibrations to match the resonance of the tone. Because it is a physical resonance, you believe it is more potent than a tone that is silently generated at the mental level.

Take a deep breath...

But again, there is no difference. It is all in the mind and how you set it up in your belief system. As you shift into the fifth dimension, you are no longer going to attract in the same way. You are simply going to manifest. You think about it; it's there. It becomes child's play.

No doubt, the third dimension is unique and quite challenging. We honor you greatly for what you are experiencing. You are doing remarkable work, and you are teaching the rest of us what compassion and integration means.

Integration

Let's continue talking about integration since it is the whole point of the experience, integration through elimination of judgments. As you go through this process of ascension, you are trying to integrate the aspects of yourself that you have not been able to "bring home", if you will, the parts of you that are still perceiving separation. As you forgive yourself for things that you have done in other lifetimes and acknowledge the wonderful things that you have also accomplished in these lives, you are erasing the barriers of separation. By doing so, your full awareness is "deposited" into your body. The full awareness says, "Ah yes, I had this lifetime and that one, and I got to play this role and that role, etc. And this is what I have learned by playing all these roles. This is what I discovered in existence." That is integration.

This is why it is so important for you to know where you are vibrating. It allows you to be in the driver's seat and not on automatic pilot. Being conscious of your vibration not only means that you can manoeuvre through reality with more grace and ease, but also you can dramatically change it by altering your frequency. Experiencing higher frequencies means more potential.

Many of you wish to know the details of your past lives so that you can integrate them. You don't have to look at past lives to do this. You simply have to look at what is going on in this lifetime. You are not recalling another lifetime to change it. Direct change can only occur in this Now moment. Sometimes when you recall a past life, what it will do is give you another perspective about the very same issues or situations that are currently being played out in this life. You might say, "Ah, I tried it that way, and that's how it worked out. And now I am repeating the same pattern."

Also know there will be many things that you will not recall, for a variety of reasons. Sometimes it is too traumatic; sometimes there are just too many details. That can create more confusion for you, so the Higher Self says, "No, never mind that. Let's focus on the Now."

In fact, a "past" life is not really past. It is going on concurrently, as remember, time does not exist. Your mastery of integration can help that lifetime. For example, in that other life you may be experiencing guilt, shame or blame. So as you learn to integrate those issues, you holographically share the process of how that integration of those issues was done with that other lifetime. This other lifetime has free will, just as you do, and can then choose to download and apply those lessons allowing for deeper healing and integration.

And here is a small bit of additional information for you: when you learn how to integrate a fear, a guilt or a blame, you send out this information to all your genetic line! How about that? They can choose to receive it and download it for learning purposes, or they can just simply file it away.

Take a deep breath...

Here is your string theory—let's take a harp. Each string has its own vibration to it, and you are constantly moving back and forth between these "strings". What you are actually doing is aligning yourself with a version of the truth that feels the best and matches your current frequency. So every fork in the road, every choice you make, can throw you onto a different string.

We give you the example of strings on a harp, but in reality, every moment you experience is a single point of focus. You link these moments together to give you the illusion of a timeline or string. All moments are Now moments. They are never past or future and are all going on concurrently. As you experience the Now, it is based on an agreed upon a set of circumstances at the personal level as well as at the collective level. You choose a point of focus, the version of the Now that you want to experience, and you project yourself into that moment. There are others who are sharing your Now moment as they are aligning with the same agreed upon set of collective circumstances.

Some of the shared information will be highlighted in your experience, and some of it will not. Let us give you an example. Many on your planet will experience wars and other highly traumatic events directly in their lives. You have agreed to be in the Now moment where the collective agreed these events would transpire, but in your personal life you are choosing to hold another resonance. That is why you are not experiencing it directly as part of your day-to-day reality. You still choose to be in this Now moment as it serves you. Your personal experience does not need to reflect all collective choices in highly dramatic ways.

Why are you creating traumatic events on the collective level? Because not enough have awakened to change it. When enough of you at the individual level choose a higher frequency, you create a template from which the collective can more readily access the information and make adjustments in their own lives.

We know, it is a bit hard for the mind to get, but that is the whole point of the mind. It is supposed to filter things out. The more you increase your vibration, the more you will begin to understand this. You don't really have to know that you are moving from focus point to focus point or Now moment to Now moment. Just know that you are moving forward and that you are choosing your potential as you advance. And know this: the past is just as flexible as the future. You can shift your experience.

Take a deep breath...

Now, we know that some of you are thinking right now, "Hmmm, if this is all an illusion and it doesn't really exist, maybe I can just deny a situation and it will eventually be released." Sorry to say, but it doesn't quite work that way. That is a thought of exclusion, which at its base is fearful. Focusing on the positive aspect of something because you want to avoid the negative will actually generate more of the negative quality because it is what you judge. That is what requires integration. Not experiencing the vibration of what you would like to deny doesn't mean that it's not there. It simply means that your focus isn't on it. You just have your back turned to it, but the judgment about it still exists. You have to include and accept it. The whole purpose of the experience is to integrate.

As multidimensional beings, you incarnate into many different dimensions at the same time. Remember, time is an illusion. Past, present and future are one. Right now, you may choose to focus your awareness on lives in one particular dimension, such as 3-D, but there are aspects of you having, say, sixth—or eighth-dimensional experiences as well. You are not relegated to the bottom of the dimensional hierarchy to work your way up. Again, you are part of source energy, and there are aspects of you having every possible experience.

Now, could this lifetime be enough to integrate all aspects of yourself? You will not get to all of them, but you will get to many of them, enough to increase your frequency to cross the dimensional barrier. Remember, it is not over because you shift. There is still more to explore and integrate in the higher realms.

We said it before—ENJOY where you are. The main premise of this game was that you were to forget. You honored that premise. Now, you are working through the heart instead of the mind. The mind kept you separate and the heart allows you to experience connection. So as you change your vibrational range to a higher frequency and you start spending more time in the operating system of the heart, the veil simply lifts. You cannot run both systems at the same time, but you can go back and forth.

We would say that this lifetime is the one that will benefit the most from integration because this is the life that is attempting to shift into the higher realms. This requires you to release all of your judgments. As we mentioned earlier, you are at the end of a grand cycle and are moving through a dense band of photonic energy. As you end one cycle and begin the next, this photonic band supports you with waves of fresh energy. These high frequency light particles support your quest to attain higher frequencies. As a result, your lower ones will get triggered. It is all part of the process.

Rewriting contracts and vows

So now, we would like to give you a simple affirmation to rewrite some of those contracts or vows that no longer serve your higher purpose. Repeat several times out loud:

I, (your name), renounce, revoke, and recall any vows, promises and contracts that are no longer in alignment with my highest good. I now revoke, renounce, recall any promises and contracts that keep me from connecting to source energy and expressing my divine self. And so it is.

This is something that you can continue to reaffirm from time to time because you do establish a few new contracts as you go. You are only dissolving the contracts that are no longer in alignment with your highest good. Don't worry, those that you have put into place and want to keep will not be altered. Besides, your Higher Self knows what to do with it all.

HEALING THE BODY

Your body is nothing more than a vibrational signature that is being pulsed out and reflected back in physical reality. Your body is created from an energetic template in your auric field. As you learn to consciously adjust your vibration, or to recalibrate, you can alter your physical state as well. Any adjustments made to the template will be reflected in the physical body.

All health issues are always, 100% of the time, created at the energetic level. Even if you have ingested something toxic or find yourself in a toxic environment, this happens because you are in resonance at the vibrational level with this frequency. If you weren't, one of two things would happen. You wouldn't encounter the toxin or it wouldn't affect your body.

Do you all get that?

Since 2010, you have been creating a new layer, or template, in your energetic field. This is the template for your higher dimensional, physical body. As you begin operating in a higher frequency range or dimension, you also run higher vibrational energy through the physical vehicle. This requires a new energetic template to hold and run the energy as well as alterations to the physical body to handle the new energy load.

We call 2011 The Year of Activation. During this time period, you began to activate more of this new energy layer. You have many labels for this new template. Some call it the Diamond Light Body or the Crystalline Body. It's all the same.

The diamond is an octahedron, two four-sided pyramids base to base. This is the shape of your new energetic vehicle and why it is called the diamond light body. A diamond is considered to be the perfect crystal, and it allows you to have a more permanent connection to source energy. When you have this light body activated, you are in tune with perfection.

Take a deep breath...

Suffice it to say that as you go through your life and increase your frequencies, you will activate this diamond light body.

Also, we encourage you to talk to your body. It loves that! The majority of you don't address your body in a positive way. Instead you say things like, "I'm fat, I'm ugly, I'm too short, too tall, too sick, etc." These are old programs that no longer serve you. When you give your body new instructions, it loves it. Think of it this way: each of your cells has a unique consciousness. They are part of the whole that is you. Don't you like to be acknowledged and appreciated? Try striking up a conversation. Just follow your own inner guidance. It will lead the way.

While we are giving you information to assist you on this journey, you are the ones going through this ascension process. You know what is best for yourselves if you quiet the mind and go within. You are teaching us about the process, as it is experience from your perspective. The experiment you agreed to undertake is one that has never been done before in such a way! We appreciate and honor that which you do.

What Kind of Diet Should I Be Following?

We are very happy and excited to talk to you about diet, health and well-being because right now you are being bombarded with so many notions of what you should be consuming. And the answer to that is there isn't one specific diet to be followed and this must be considered on an individual basis. It is, at the end of the day, about energy levels and frequency.

What's important to understand is that you are pure energy, a being of light and frequency. When we talk about diet, health and well-being, there are two levels from which to view the issue. First, you can look at it from a very physical point of view, but that's only going to take you so far. The second is from an energetic standpoint. So, let us start with the physical and then move on to our perspective of the energetic.

When considering the type and quality of food to consume (organic, conventional, raw, cooked, animal products), requirements are based upon the individual. Ideally, you should be eating fresh, organically grown produce and animals that have been treated with love and respect. Some of you, however, have viewed the slaughter of animals on your planet and decided that no animal product should be consumed in any manner, under any circumstance. Well, we will tell you this belief is most often fueled by judgment. We know that some of you are not going to agree; that is fine, too. We are simply offering another perspective on this subject.

At a purely physical level, there is sometimes still the need for you to consume animal meat from time to time. You need the minerals and the protein as well as some of the complex strands of molecules that come only from animal sources as you are recalibrating and upgrading your cellular structures.

Whether you choose to eat plants or meat, we do recommend that you do so with a respect for nature and value the life you are consuming, giving thanks for its existence. You are absorbing the life force energy of another consciousness. But we will speak a bit more to that as we get into the energy aspects of it, all right.

When you eat too much of anything, even healthy foods, they are no longer healthy. It's all about balance and moderation across the board. So that's what we would like you to focus on.

Currently, there are many foods that have been introduced into the mainstream that have been genetically modified. When food is genetically altered, you lose not only some of the energetic qualities of the foods, but also the nutritional value. You can alter the harmonics of the energetic resonance, but you can't really add the nutrients back in. It is best to consume a variety of natural, non-modified foods that have been grown in rich soil without toxic chemicals, allowing for a more balanced intake. Taking packaged vitamins and minerals is not quite the same thing as eating high-quality foods that contain those vitamins and minerals because of this energetic resonance. Due to extraction methods and packaging, most vitamins and minerals out there will lose their energetic component. While you are getting some energy on the physical level, the vibrational quality of your food is never quite the same as when it is grown with love from non-modified seeds.

Should you be eating all carbs or all protein? Of course not. Rather, it's a little bit of everything. You've got to listen to your own body. Intuitively you will know what nutrients you need, and you will be drawn to foods that contain them. Animals do this as well. When they are ill, they know they need to eat certain foods, and the same goes for you. But the whole notion of diet and the connotation that word has these days is that of restriction for weight management rather than a regimen for health and vitality. And when we are talking about the issue of weight, we are talking about something vastly different than health.

Cells can retain fluids and other biological matter for a number of reasons. It can be for protection. It can also be caused by an imbalance in the cells. If this is the case, the cells are unable to release because they are missing the chemical components they need to function properly. Besides overeating, there are many other factors that can contribute to weight gain, which brings us to the emotional or energetic component. From our point of view, it is far more important and has a greater impact on your diet and health than anything else.

Holding onto weight, keeping your body from purifying itself or consuming foods that are not of the highest vibration, sometimes serves you. You may have a belief or emotion in place that draws you to these scenarios. For example, you may have a belief or an emotional issue around safety. By eating pure foods, the body can release toxins and weight that numb you and keep you from feeling these unsafe feelings. By detoxing, you become more sensitive to frequency. Unless you are ready to deal with the belief or emotion, you will continue to be drawn to foods and habits that suppress them.

That's why sometimes it's very difficult, although you've set the intention, for you to get on a healthy regimen where you are consuming high-quality foods; emotionally you are not prepared to let go of issues. By being lighter, you are going to be more in tune with your body and your emotional states. If you are not prepared to deal with those emotions, chances are you are not going to allow the physical to lighten up. You don't want to deal with it! So in those cases, you've got to go and look at what's going on emotionally. And we are not talking about issues that are necessarily tied to food and diet. We are talking about everything across the board; in your relationships, in your perceptions of yourself and what you are doing in life. You can't separate the two. Again, this is a very important notion we want to get across to you.

If we have lost you here, let us back up and see if we can make sure that this is crystal clear because this is very important for you to understand. You attract to yourself exactly what you need. It is the Law of Attraction. When you are ready to move forward and release an emotional issue, you will start eating healthier foods intuitively/subconsciously. You begin eating healthy foods because of a change in mind set and/or an emotional pattern. Your body will begin to release what it was previously told to hold onto, allowing you to raise the frequency of the cells. If you are doing this on an unconscious level, there is part of you that says, "You know what? I am ready to move forward." You start to eat smaller meals. You start to eat healthier food. And guess what? Emotions start to come up so you can deal with them.

You, too, vibrate at specific frequency ranges. When you are happy and healthy, you are at the top of the range. When you are holding negative emotions in your energetic field or your body is processing a heavy toxic load, you are vibrating at a much lower rate.

One of the many special attributes of this planet is the vast range of diversity in all aspects of life—food being one of the most diverse due to the wide range of plant life here. It is, in fact, quite rare among planets. Each plant holds a unique frequency, thus you are able to ascertain the medicinal properties of them. You've got a wide variety, which makes your culinary experiments, your cuisines, something very, very special. We hear some can be quite wonderful, like ice cream and cookies, for example.

When you put those things into your body, it takes a certain amount of energy to process them out. So you are lowering your frequency. But if you have such an emotional attachment to those foods and you really want to have that pleasure but you continually deny yourself, the negative emotion that builds up is far more detrimental to your body and overall frequency than if you had had the cookie or ice cream and processed the toxins out. So you've got to find a balance there. Denying yourself, or simply the constant perception of denial, can do more damage than actually having the food. This is also important for you to know and understand.

That's just a taste of what is going on with your diet. As you change and begin to grow spiritually, most of you will not be drawn to the animal products quite as much, as their frequency is a bit lower than that of plants. When it comes to animals, the manner in which they lived and perished is locked into the frequency of their molecules. You are absorbing and "accessing", if you will, its life experience. It is one of your few intimate connections to Earth and her rhythm of life. If you are eating animals that have been tormented or their death was quite traumatic, their frequency is far lower than an animal that has had a happy lifetime.

We've gone a bit around here in a circle and this is, in part, how we like to work with you. We don't want you to be thinking in too linear a fashion. We want to start to get you thinking multidimensionally. So we hope we haven't lost you here, dears.

The last thing we want to discuss is how to work with food if it has been genetically modified or you are not certain of its origin. You can alter the frequency of the food by sending it energy, love and good vibrations. This releases the negative emotional component that is locked into the physical cells so as not to be taken into the body upon consumption. This is the notion of blessing your food. By giving thanks for it, by giving it energy, by giving it positive feelings of love and gratitude, you can alter the structure of the cellular resonance. This is one practice you can follow for both food and water to lighten the vibrational load on the body.

HOW TO BEST DEAL WITH NEWS, WARS, DEATH AND DESTRUCTION

The news

We would say that it is important to have awareness of your environment, but more importantly what you perceive in your environment shows you where your personal vibration is. As you become aware of what is going on collectively, it is a reflection of what is going on with you at the microcosmic level. Remember, you operate under the Laws of Attraction and Reflection. If something is not in alignment with you in any way, shape or form, you will probably never hear about it. And if you do, it will not have any effect on you.

The important piece to take away when watching or reading the news is an awareness of your judgments. Where are your thoughts, feelings and emotions when it comes to the story? If you are feeling angry, frustrated or even apathetic, it is an opportunity for you to do some inner work, to let go of any fears or lower vibrational thoughts that you are carrying.

Let us give you an example. Perhaps you heard in the news a story about bankers, and even though you are not directly involved in the situation, you feel yourself become activated and angry. You feel that you don't have any control or power over what is going on. We would say, "Where else do you feel powerless? Where is this scenario being played out in your life? Where in your life do you feel like a victim?"

We guarantee you that you are playing this game in multiple areas of your own life. Your reaction to the story is an indicator that the programs are there. Now because of the reflection, you have an opportunity to identify the frequency and integrate it. Look carefully at how that belief or thought serves you. When you recognize the pattern, you can then shift it. Maybe at another time in your life, this thought or pattern did serve you and kept you safe, but it may not serve you any longer. If this is the case, are you willing to let it go? An awareness such as this is the difference between being in the driver's seat vibrationally or being on automatic pilot.

When you see the service of any thought, pattern or belief, you move out of the victim/perpetrator mentality and move into the co-creator level of awareness. When you do this, you let go of any attachment or judgment. It immediately happens. It is only in the mindset of the victim/ perpetrator that judgment can exist. At the co-creator level, all are acceptable experiences. They aren't good or bad. There is not one that is better to have over another. As co-creators, you all sought out and experienced these varied frequencies and roles.

The news is also an opportunity to identify where the collective consciousness is vibrating. Again, you are not bound to play out the frequencies of collective consciousness. You can hold your own unique frequency. But if you feel charged in anyway, it means that you still have work to do. You are not a victim!

Remember, when you shift your frequency, you holographically transmit the information on how it was done to the collective consciousness. Others may then access this information if they so choose. You give people who are struggling assistance and reassurance that it can be done by simply being the living example.

One of the major issues that you may see in the news revolves around the idea of competition. The third-dimensional perspective says it is either this or it is that. It is one or the other. One country wins a war; the other loses. You either have prosperity or lack, with nothing in between. These stories keep you in separation. What we encourage you to understand is that it is not about "either/or", but rather "and". The Universe is infinitely abundant, so there truly is no limitation or lack except that which is self-imposed. You can have your own beliefs without the need for others to conform. All can succeed and flourish.

When you move into higher frequencies of awareness, you see that everyone has the possibility to thrive. There are no victims. Many of you get frustrated when you hear us say this. You say, "Why would anybody choose poverty, war or famine? How could they choose this particular version of reality?" The reason is simple; they wanted to explore a frequency. Honor them for their choice as a divine being of light. Hold for them the wisdom that they may choose to see themselves from a higher perspective. You can send them energy encoded with the knowledge that they can choose to increase their frequency and experience more love.

Ascension is not a requirement. If others do not wish to awaken, it does not tie you into that reality. You experience that reality because that is YOUR choice. When you decide to move out of the mode of victim/perpetrator, you can create a life of joy, abundance and expansion no matter what the collective may be choosing.

Wars, death and destruction

We often hear you ask, "Why is there so much war and death in the world? Why aren't people doing more to stop it?" Again, you are playing in a game of descension and reascension, and the illusion of separation.

Know that much of what is going on in the news is being manufactured. You are being told versions of the stories that often do not include the whole truth. Remember, we told you earlier that truth is always colored by perspective. This is an opportunity to use your discernment. So ask yourselves, "Is this truth in alignment with me?". If the answer is no, then you can start to verbalize that—not for the purpose of confrontation, but rather as a way of expressing your desire to create reality with a higher vibration. You don't have to fight your governments. You just have to say I want peace. If you hold focus and take action, that is in alignment with that higher desire, and that desire will be reflected in your reality. Anything you wish to fight against or to eradicate is, in fact, something you are judging. You will continue to receive that which you judge as your reflection so that it may be brought to your awareness and integrated.

The reason why on the surface so many of you "appear" to be callous and not get involved in changing the state of the world is in part because you have shut down your heart centers. This is usually due to a tremendous lack of self-love, fear of hurt, blame or shame. Because that part of you is closed off, it is very difficult for you to have compassion.

Now, concerning death, know that everyone who has gone through a death cycle has done so willingly. There is not a single person on the planet who has died that did not do everything they wanted to do in this life as it was. We guarantee you, if there was anything else that they wanted to do, they would have done it.

How an individual goes through the death cycle, how they die, determines not only the vibrational experience for themselves, but also sets up an experience for those around them. Let us give you an example. A 90-year-old man passes in his sleep. You all may say, "Ah, he lived a long, full life. Good for him." But if an individual dies at the age of 20, you may say, "Ah, he was much too young! It should never have happened." The perceptions and judgments surrounding the manner and age of death can create vastly different experiences for those remaining on Earth. If a loved one is murdered, that can set up programs of revenge or fear of safety. Suicides can trigger feelings of abandonment or guilt. Even in death, you co-create with others.

We always say, "Drama happens when you aren't paying attention TO GET your attention." When many die through a war or mass disaster, it can be perceived as a tragedy, but also as a gift bestowed upon the collective. Those who die choose to depart in such a manner and in such numbers not only for their own personal experience, but also to awaken the collective consciousness to an issue. It is an opportunity to choose a new vibration, release fears and attachments, and to move into a higher frequency. It is an opportunity that, unfortunately, most of you don't take. The general tendency for most is to blame. If you can observe the situation as a service, it automatically puts you in your heart center and allows you to process similar frequencies in your own field. We encourage you to look at some of the current wars or disasters. Ask yourself:

- What is the event really about?
- Is it about competition and control? Safety? Security? Lack? Trust?
- Where do I play out these issues in my own life?

Start clearing at the personal level. Remember, what you see reflected in the collective is there within you. Personal integration helps to create global change as you are no longer perpetuating that scenario.

Currently, the collective creates wars and conflicts by trying to obtain what others have because they fear there is not enough to go around. They believe in lack rather than infinite abundance. As you increase your collective frequency, you will begin to move into a state where everyone's needs are met. In fact, your focus will no longer be on your personal needs but rather on how you can best be of service. From this space of infinite abundance, you trust that all your needs will be met without ever truly focusing directly on them. We know you find this difficult to even fathom at this time because you are not operating in an unconditional way on the planet. As we told you, we are here to give you another perspective on how to dissolve the illusion.

We offer you this simple affirmation: *I stand in peace in the midst of chaos.* No matter what is going on with the collective, you can generate your own unique experience. In times of war, you can create great peace in your personal life. In times of financial upset, you can create limitless abundance. You can experience love, wealth, connection, passion and excitement all on your own. As you hold these frequencies, you become a way-shower for others who may not be able to find them for themselves.

As you radiate tremendous amounts of love and joy around you, there will be those willing to increase their frequencies to join you. But again, remember, they don't have to. The idea that all should want to increase their frequency goes back to judgment and the idea of competition. You may hold a fearful belief that those who do increase their frequency are better than those who don't or that somehow you are not able to live a life of joy and love because others are unwilling to do so themselves. Not at all.

Be the living example.

THE LOVE OF YOUR LIFE... IS YOU.

All of your relationships are founded on self-love, which is then reflected back to you through these relationships. We consider lack of self-love the number one issue on the planet at this time, closely followed by persecution in second. We really want to make this point clear: it is not about your relationships with others, but first and foremost the relationship you have with self that will allow you to access more love, joy, happiness, abundance, health and vitality. This is a major core issue for you, and we wish to assist you in shifting your perspective.

There are many programs in mass consciousness that keep you locked into lack of self-love. We are going to talk about some of them here. The first one that we have quite a bit of trouble with because it sets you up for failure and separation is the idea of what you call soul mates and twin flames. We are not saying that they do not exist, but what we are saying is that it is an extremely rare occurrence in this particular lifetime. Even if you choose not to work with a soul mate or twin flame, it really doesn't matter because the relationship with a twin flame or a soul mate is no different than any other relationship that you can create for yourself. It was a label that you put on relationships at a time when you did not have the potential to interact with as many people as you do today due to your ability to travel and connect via the Internet.

The idea of a twin flame or soul mate sets you all up with the notion that there is only one person with whom you can experience love, and if you don't meet this person you are missing out. This lifetime more than any other you are focused on integrating as many aspects of yourself as possible. One way to accomplish this is to work with those with whom you have unresolved issues in other lifetimes. The more relationships you have, the better your chances to integrate, some of which may be romantic relationships.

Within a relationship, there are about 100 points of vibrational connection that you can establish. In most long-term relationships, about thirty of these points align. In most short-term relationships, you work with about 10. In this lifetime, you are able to work through these issues pretty quickly, whereas in other times in history, the pace of integration was much slower as the overall vibration was much lower. It took you much longer to identify the lower programs that were running. In the past, you may have chosen to only work on four or five big issues in a lifetime. Relationships tended to last a bit longer as it took you a while to see these issues, and you typically had a smaller pool of people to interact with to be reflections for you. Remember, at this time you have more universal support as you move through the photon band. These high vibrational particles assist you in the process of integration so you are able to work faster and with a greater range of frequencies.

Today, because the pace is accelerated, you are trying to integrate as much as you possibly can. What you may find is that before you incarnated, you set up contracts for potential relationships. For instance, you had persons A, B and C lined up as possible romantic relationships. If A wasn't ready, then you had B as a backup. If A and B weren't available, you moved on to C and so on. You set up your contracts this way because timing is far more challenging in this lifetime. The potential for you to integrate is much greater and as you do so, the need to connect, or the attraction to connect with a specific individual, will shift.

Most of you hold the belief that contracts are eternally binding and difficult to change. On the contrary, they are very malleable. You think of them as "heavy" and that if you don't show up at a particular time or place, you are missing out on an opportunity. That comes from fear, lack, distrust and disconnection. You never, ever miss an opportunity. If you are pulsing out frequency, it will be reflected back to you. It is just a matter of whether you are open to perceive and receive it. The form could be slightly different to that of the opportunity you passed on initially, but the frequency that you want to experience will be identical to the original.

This is very important because often times in relationships, you tend to focus on a particular person as opposed to staying open to form. When you are open to form, the person who is the best vibrational match for you can show up. Discomfort arises when you get stuck on, or attached to, a person who is not the highest vibrational match for you. Attachment will always create discomfort.

Take a nice breath...

Indeed, you have many individuals with whom you have contracted. Again, your desire to have a twin flame on this planet is a little damaging. Know that you can experience amazing, wondrous connections with absolutely everyone and everything when you start to run programs of self-love. The more you connect with source, the more love you have for yourself and all others.

Many of you are afraid to connect with others because you are afraid you will connect with their dysfunction. But as you start elevating your frequency and connecting more with source, you start to connect to your own divine self and, as a reflection, you will begin to connect to the divinity in others. As you do so, every relationship can start to feel like a loving relationship. It doesn't have to be difficult. It doesn't have to be a struggle. The difficulties and struggles come from fear programs, and these are all illusionary. The more you stay present, the more you can identify those programs and decide in the moment not to judge. You will be able to change what you are pulsing out and dramatically alter your relationships. In your love relationships, you all tend to go back to memories of the past, making assumptions that this moment will be identical to a previous one, thus repeating the same old patterns. You use your past experience as a point of reference rather than simply being present and allowing the moment to be new and unique. You say to yourself, "This is what happened to me in the past, and it is just going to happen to me again." How many of you have had that thought?

As you change the relationship that you have with yourself, your old programming, you will then change the relationships that you have with others. Others do not have to change their behavior in order for you to alter the dynamics of a relationship. This is true for all manner of relationships including a family member, a coworker, a lover, a friend, etc. Like attracts like.

So as you start changing your programming, if others in your entourage are still running the old programs, which are no longer a match for yours, they won't be able to play them out with you. They may play the old programs out with others, but again, not with you. Remember, only when there is a vibrational attraction do you co-create.

Right now, you are entering a period of creation of form like never before. We encourage you to focus on frequency—joy, abundance, self-love, harmony, etc. It is all about the essence of creation and not about what it should look like. By focusing on frequency rather than form, you are releasing the burden of expectation and the desire for the connection outside of you—like looking for your other half, the one that is supposed to complete you!

This is very strong in your social construct, and women have a more challenging time with that because of social conditioning. Why? For the last several thousand years, women have been socially conditioned to believe that their only value is as a wife and mother. Beyond that, women are not suppose to want anything more or different. As a result of those beliefs, if you are not in a relationship, you have less value or something is wrong with you. That is why self-love is so important.

For men, the conditioning is a little different. Value is placed on work and money. If you lack money or are unemployed, self-worth issues come to the surface. Generally speaking, for men it is about ascertaining what is tangible; for woman, it is about emotional connection. Women get locked into the idea of wanting a relationship and men have a challenging time expressing emotions since from a very young age, they often are taught to suppress them.

Take a nice deep breath...

Self-love is something that you already carry within. It is not something that you have to achieve, but rather, you simply dissolve the illusionary programs and filters that prevent you from experiencing more of that self-love. The reflections that you receive through your relationships in the world will show you what programs still need to be integrated.

We can tell you what self-love looks like in the physical body—radiant health. If you are giving yourself self-love, you are giving yourself source energy. The cells are able to maintain health and vitality because they are receiving high frequency energy. The physical body is created by the energetic template so any ailment in the physical body is a reflection of a lower frequency in your energetic template. Check in at the emotional level. If you are feeling any lower emotions like anxiety, depression, anger or fear, there is a lack of self-love going on. At the mental level, if your inner critic is expressing any negative thoughts like, "I'm not good enough," or "I don't deserve this," that is the opposite of loving self. You are not accessing the self-love that is contained in you.

For the last 25 years, you have been told that it is time to reawaken. Well, we would like to help you with the "practice" of reawakening. It is something that you have to keep doing on a day-to-day basis, hour by hour, minute to minute and eventually moment to moment. This is our focus in 2013.

Many of you will find excuses not to practice, often pretending that you are too busy. Are you really too busy to love yourself? Knowing the theory is one thing, but practicing and implementing it into moment-to-moment reality is another. Practice simply means being aware at any given moment of where you are vibrating at the mental, emotional and physical levels and making adjustments, releasing judgment, and allowing more love to flow.

Maintaining frequency is another aspect of creation that we have not yet discussed. You see, when you pulse out frequency, you must be vibrating at the same rate in order to receive it in physical form. You cannot pulse out a high frequency and receive it when you are vibrating at a lower rate. You must be in the same vibrational space. They both have to be aligned. If they are, you are going to receive what you asked for. If you find that what you requested isn't showing up, have appreciation for what is. Consider it a gift. What is directly in front of you shows you your conscious and subconscious programs. As you integrate these, you can elevate your frequency to match that which you seek to create.

In order to change where you are, you have to accept where you are. If you keep pushing away that thing that you don't want, what you are doing in reality is charging yourself to it. When you open up, acknowledge that low frequency without pushing it away, and have appreciation for it, you neutralize the charge. You are no longer playing the game of victim/perpetrator. Once you do that, the issue is dissolved.

Relationships

Many of you who have chosen to awaken at this time have decided not to have long-term relationships for a number of reasons. For many, it was important for you to find your identity and be clear about your own energy. Thus, you placed your focus on self. Had you been in a relationship, the dynamic would have been very different. Following a "traditional" path can make it easier to plug into mass consciousness and all the beliefs that come with that.

As you increase your frequency, some of the programming around isolation and avoidance of intimate relationships is coming to an end. With the upshift in energies following 2012, contracts of that nature have changed as you are activating the 5-D programs. It will be vital to work on self-love in order to experience the kind of deep, meaningful relationships you seek. To create a relationship that stems from a higher consciousness perspective, you have to work on the integration of masculine and feminine within. Again, this requires you to first and foremost establish a connection with self. You have no choice. Those in your external reality are simply there to add to your physical experience. They don't complete it. They don't define it. The connection that you are seeking is with source energy and to experience that, you have to connect with self first.

Generally speaking, in an intimate relationship you are more open and that openness and willingness to feel love brings you closer to source energy. That amazing sense of bliss and love that you feel is not there because of the other person. It is coming from you! How's that for a mind bender? You are feeling more of what source energy is, and it happened because you were willing to open. But when that relationship ends, you think that you will never experience that sense of bliss again. It is possible through self-love and openness to receive? Can you experience that feeling of bliss without a partner? Absolutely! You will feel it not only towards another person in partnership but towards everyone and everything.

Our purpose is to help you find that self-love. Start by writing a letter about what you appreciate about yourself, your qualities and your kindnesses. Would you be afraid to tell someone you love what you think about them? So why not do it for yourself?

Now take your qualities or the appreciation for those qualities and focus on them. Those qualities are in your energetic field and when you can show more appreciation for them, it will help you create more of these qualities in your life. You just have to feel them in your body instead of having your inner critic tell you that you are not good enough, you are not lovable or not smart enough, etc. But when you stop and focus your energy on what you appreciate, you will get more of these things in your life. Most importantly, your inner critic will have less time to give you those negative thoughts.

What will happen after a week of this? Your interaction with other people will be vastly different because, once again, they will be the reflection of you loving yourself. For example, if one of the qualities that you focus on is peacefulness, you will find that people will say things like, "I feel very peaceful and calm when I am in your presence," or if someone is very agitated, when he comes in contact with your energy field, he will become more peaceful. If one of your qualities is being a loving person, then what you will see is more opportunities for being loving and you will have people come into your field that also will be more loving because that is where your focus is.

What we are inviting you to do is to work the 5-D way instead of the 3-D. There is a part of the human mind that will not release until a conscious awareness is present. Once you have that, you can let it go if you choose. It is part of the construct of the game that you have set up for yourselves. That is the 3-D model. The 5-D model of creation is alignment with frequency. So by working with the 5-D model, you are simply realigning yourself with the essence of what you want. That is in part what we are guiding you towards by pulling out those qualities that you want and that you appreciate in yourself. This will help you put less attention on things you don't want. You are now able, because you have elevated your frequency, to activate the inner technology of 5-D creation.

We are going to walk you through that inner technology of creation.

- First, think about something that you would like to create.
- Now, what is the essence of it? What is the frequency of it? (Meaning what does it represent vibrationally—freedom, joy, excitement, stability?)
- Then, what we'd like you to do is to imagine yourself aligning with the frequency in your physical body. You don't have to think when or where, just be in alignment with the essence of what you want.

This model of creation is much easier because you are working with frequency and not a mental image of the form. Remember, you are a vibrational being. In 5-D, you are simply removing the mental component. So if you want to create change in your life, we would say to start here, with a love letter to yourself, and see what happens.

We challenge you to do this for the next seven days by spending 10 minutes every morning writing yourself a new love letter. Then, focus on the frequencies of the qualities that you have written in that love letter.

If there is resistance, you can go back to the 3-D model of visualizing the form. If you find you don't want to write yourself a love letter, ask yourself why you are resisting. To keep safe from accessing more of your power or more love? Is it a control issue? Noting the source of your resistance will show you what lower frequency programs you are running.

The natural flow of all things is toward source. So if something is difficult, there is resistance. If you are in divine flow, it is easy, easy, easy.

Obligations

Now, we want you to list five obligations that you have. For example, you may feel obligated to call a parent every day, or maybe you feel obligated to have lunch every week with a certain friend. It could be something in the present, past or future.

Once your list is done, we would like you to consider saying no to that obligation. When it comes to doing something out of obligation, we would say either not to do it or you have to reframe your perception of it. Know that when you agree to do something and the intention underneath is of a lower frequency, meaning there is resistance in doing it or it makes you unhappy, that is what is going to be created in reality—a low vibration experience.

Let's take an example of the lunch with a friend. If you don't want to go for any reason, then you simply cancel or you reframe it by finding something that you can appreciate and love about that person and/or your lunch date. This makes a big difference in the vibrational outcome and what you experience.

This is a big piece with working with self-love. Doing something that you don't want to do takes such a huge amount of energy that it prevents you from nourishing yourself. This is part of your conditioning, especially for women. You think that you have to give, give, give, and you end up energetically bankrupt.

So it is very important that you look at the obligations that you have set up. When you go through with something that you don't want to do, you are not honoring yourself. This not only includes obligations in relationship to others, but also obligations you place on yourself like going to the gym because you feel that you should. Diet is also a big one, especially around being a vegetarian. There is a lot of superiority programming there, but also programs around deprivation. Honor what your body asks for.

Money is another a big issue. Money is nothing more than energy. Are you worried about money in your life, and what does it represent to you? It is usually what money represents that you need to focus on. Is it freedom, creativity, status or worthiness? If you lack money, what is it that you are denying yourself and why? A fear program is present. If you truly loved and nourished yourself, you would allow yourself the experience of having infinite abundance and that includes money. So think about that.

The more loving you are with yourself, the more loving you can be with everyone and everything. If you don't do that, you will find yourself very tired and running in circles. We know this is not always an easy thing to look at, and we applaud you for doing so.

We are so very excited for you, and we really want to acknowledge your willingness to look inside of you to find that self-love first and foremost because all things are created from that point.

CONVERSATION WITH THE NINTH-DIMENSIONAL PLEIADIANS

The Universal Game — Post 2012

In the information concerning the grand experiment, you say, "that we are also at the end of a universal cycle and when this process of integration is shared with the Universe, it will change it so dramatically that the game will be finished."

If I understand correctly, our 26,000-year cycle was about our life in the Now amongst the process of integration. The universal game is about all our other lives being transformed by this one life.

— For the game to be over, wouldn't all the lives of all the beings in the Universe, some of which never even incarnated on Earth, be integrated?

Not entirely. As humans you tend to think in finite terms, and it is an infinite Universe. The end of a universal cycle simply means that you are shifting focus and implementing a new set of rules, new players or new challenges to the game. It is the same thing that you experience on the smaller scale with your astrology as you move through the signs of the zodiac. You have a sequence of general trends that you wish to experience, and so it is with universal cycles as well.

The human mind fears that the end of a cycle means that it will cease to exist because that is how you perceive your life on the planet. You think you cease to exist when you die, so you try to apply the same logic to the universal game. Neither works that way. You are an infinite being and as such will continue to infinitely expand and contract. Never do you cease to exist.

At source level, all are integrated. In order to complete a cycle, it does not mean that all beings everywhere must have an awareness of their expanded self. Those of you on Earth were playing a game of descension and reascension, which meant you, from your limited perspective of self and separation, needed to have an understanding of yourself as a universal being of light having a human experience. You didn't need to access all those lifetimes consciously. Your goal was to release as much judgment and as many perceptions of separation as possible until you increased your frequency enough to cross the dimensional barrier, which you have accomplished.

You are currently residing in the fourth dimension. It is one of transition and highly malleable, which allows you to apply either third-dimensional or fifth-dimensional rules of perception and creation to it. The third and fifth dimensions have very fixed rules to the dimensional structure and because they are so different, you needed a whole dimension to adjust to shifting between them. Most of you have no awareness that you have shifted because you are still applying the 3-D principles to the 4-D matrix. But what you are beginning to play with is the application of 5-D rules on the 4-D matrix. Eventually you will be ready to fully immerse yourselves in the 5-D version, and at that point you will shift out of the fourth dimension and into the fifth.

As you have gone through this process of ascension, each of you has entered his or her own unique procedure for integration, which includes compassion and the release of judgment, into the universal records. All beings then have access to the information if they so choose to receive and/or retrieve it. You can think of it a bit like discovering a new route to a destination. You can continue to take the old, winding dirt path, or you can choose the new, paved direct route.

It is your choice, but most would choose the new direct route. And so it is. Many will access compassion in a new way, and it will forever color their perspective of everything they experience. Once you learn something, it is rather difficult to "unknow" it. But we must say, you all are pretty good at giving it a go in 3-D. It is also why 3-D is such a special dimension. It is unlike any other in that you get to experience the illusion of separation, which allows you to "forget" some things. We will say forget, but you never really do. You simply choose not to access certain files or memories.

All benefit from the unique experience of a single individual, but when enough of you experience or create similar vibrational frequencies, it amplifies the signature, broadcasting it and making it easily available to many. You can think of it like a radio signal being broadcast. Once the volume is up, more people can hear the broadcast. The stronger the signal, the farther it can be sent.

—How is the galactic community affected by the end of our cycle?

With the end of a universal cycle, all beings have an opportunity to complete issues that they have been working on. Different systems and dimensions all have unique games running. With Earth's ascension and as you continue to learn and integrate non-judgment, those in other sectors of your galaxy also have access to this information and will most directly benefit from your experience with the close of this galactic cycle. As Earth is a grand experiment, you are playing out many of the galactic issues at the individual and collective, planetary level. What many of you consider to be your galactic family are other aspects of you, and as you learn how to integrate, those other aspects of you too can access and apply that information. Let us give you an example. In the Lyran star system, you may be feline and you find distaste and judgment for others who are not of your species. On Earth, you may be one who has released judgment about others who were not the same race or creed as you. That information is transmitted to all aspects of you. So the feline aspect can then apply the lesson. Your feline aspect may suddenly find him or herself perceiving other species in a new and open way, without ever having a conscious awareness that the human version of you deposited wisdom and knowledge into their energetic field.

Judgment Versus Forgiveness

Elimination of judgment and forgiveness are two ways of letting go. But from what I understand, forgiveness is not quite the same thing as no judgment. When you forgive, you can still have judgment about a situation. It can help you get out of anger or deception and go forward, but it can still include judgment. Many times we hear people say, "I can forgive but I never forget."

—Is forgiveness the first step toward no judgment or is it a completely different energy?

You are currently operating under the universal Laws of Attraction and Reflection. As part of the construct of the 3-D game, you knew that it would be difficult from the perception of limitation to see and recognize frequency within yourself, so the universal Laws of Attraction and Reflection were put into place. Your reality and all that you perceive in it is a reflection of your vibrational frequency.

You are creating and generating 100% of your reality 100% of the time. Not just *SOME* times. At *ALL* times, at *ALL* levels, what you label as good and bad. Neither really exists as such. They are simply vibrational experiences.

Any time you perceive yourself as a perpetrator or a victim, you are perceiving reality through the operating system of the mind. The mind was created as a construct that allows for the perception of limitation, separation and linear time; in other words, it is where you run your ego programs or filters that color your perception of reality. The heart is the operating system for the multidimensional self in which you run none of the ego programs or filters and can perceive and understand the true nature of reality as a universal being of light generating a human experience. At this level, you are aware that there is no time, you are connected to everyone and everything, and your experiences are co-created by you, another consciousness and source. This is the true nature of your holy trinity. All things in form hold consciousness so co-creation can occur with nature, animals or other beings. In a dualistic Universe of which you are a part, there must be a polar opposite to each experience. In other words, you must have a perpetrator for each victim. Ah, we already hear some of you asking, "If the Universe is dualistic, does that mean you have victims and perpetrators in 9-D? No, we choose to play our polarity out in other ways. Different dimensions have different constructs. From the fifth-dimensional level up, we do not perceive ourselves as being separate from anyone or anything, so we know we co-create and operate with that as our basic premise. We may not always agree, but we do know reality is of our own making.

If you are still seeing yourself as a victim, then you are not taking responsibility for your part of co-creation. When you see the service of your co-creations, what it teaches or reminds you, then you are able to move beyond victimization and truly forgive and forget.

If you have not forgotten, then you haven't forgiven. We would say this is true about 99% of the time. You are still referencing a hurt. You perceive yourself as victimized in some way and you are still going back to that moment in time. If you have forgiven, then you will most likely not think about a scenario unless you encounter the same frequency again and recall past moments when you previously experienced it. And if it is being reflected back to you in your reality, then there is something in your field that you are holding and pulsing out that is creating and generating that reflection.

We will also say this to you: any time you are not in the present moment, you are in the operating system of the mind, which again means you are perceiving things from a fear-based, limited perspective. If you are fully engaged with the present Now moment, it is impossible to reference the past. The moment you disengage from the Now, you move out of the operating system of the heart and are back in the operating system of the mind.

We can see many of you don't really like this answer, but it is the true nature of things. It feels more comfortable and safe to go back to the illusion of the mind where you take only partial or no responsibility.

So yes, real forgiveness means no judgment. Period! If you are still judging it in any way, you haven't truly forgiven.

As with any fear, you may choose to process it in levels and layers. For most of you to bring up all the perceived pain with a fear would leave you in a heap on the floor, so you will only reveal to yourself as much as you are prepared to process. And how do you process? When you have the awareness you are still harboring ill feelings, check in with yourself and see what is going on at the physical, mental and emotional level. Does your body go into contraction? If so, what is the thought or emotion that signals the body to do so? What is going on at the mental level? What are your thoughts? Perhaps the mind says, "You fool, you can't forgive. You are gullible and naïve if you do that!" How are you feeling emotionally? Insecure? Fearful? If you are feeling anything but total peace at all levels with an issue or experience, then there is more judgment to be released or integrated. You must move into the heart center to do this. It is impossible to release from the level of the mind. It is possible that you may have forgiven at the mental level, but you haven't dealt with the emotional component of it or vice versa. Again, all levels must be addressed to fully release judgment.

If you are having difficulty finding forgiveness, then we recommend you take a look at where you are playing out that very same frequency with another person or perhaps in another area of your life. We guarantee you are playing it out in multiple ways. It may look different on the surface, but the base thought, feeling or emotion is the same. As you integrate or release the judgment of a frequency in one area of your life, you release it in all areas.

As an example, perhaps you have had a difficult time throughout your life forgiving a parent for their poor child-rearing skills. You felt abandoned. Now as an adult, you are experiencing that same frequency of abandonment but from another perspective. In the current moment, you are not receiving as much attention and support as you would hope for from your boss. Your abandonment is once again triggered. This time, because the scenario is slightly different, you are able to perceive it from another perspective. You are able to see your boss is not there to hold your hand, so you decide to stand in your power, make a few key decisions on your own, and proceed forward with your project. Doing so allows you to see that you are capable of more than you gave yourself credit for initially and you no longer align with the belief that you were abandoned but that it was an opportunity for you to stretch your wings. By clearing the sense of abandonment with the boss, you automatically apply the same integration to the issue with the parent. You may now find when you reflect on your parent, you no longer hold the anger or resentment or, at the very least, not to the same degree that you once did.

— When we change our timelines, there is a completely different set of circumstances. But we are, at one point or the other, sharing the same dot or general consciousness with a version of humanity, but we are also, each of us, on individual timelines having different experiences. So If I understand correctly, we all decided to play, for a while, the same game and be on the same dots but experiencing different circumstances?

When we talk about time, it is important that you move out of the head and into the heart. Typically when the topic comes up about the multidimensional perspective of time, it puts you all first in your heads and then second out of your bodies because it makes you very uncomfortable. The information does not compute with the logical mind and your current perception of reality. You will never find the answer for the multidimensional perspective in the mind. The mind was designed to throw out the multidimensional perspective. That was the whole purpose of it, so that you could have a unique experience of separation and linear time. You have to be in your heart center to process this. So as we talk about it, as we give you the information, see it as an orb of light dropping from the mind down into your heart and try processing it there. When you are in the heart center, things will make more sense. If you're in the head, forget about it. You're going to go crazy like a hamster on a wheel going around and around and around.

The illusion of time is probably one of the most important concepts for you all to grasp moving forward. Remember what we give to you as an explanation is not the whole truth, but it is the version of the truth that you can comprehend in this moment as you are playing still in the illusion of time. How you move out of the illusion and into the reality of multidimensional existence is an amazing adventure and one that we are excited to see you take.

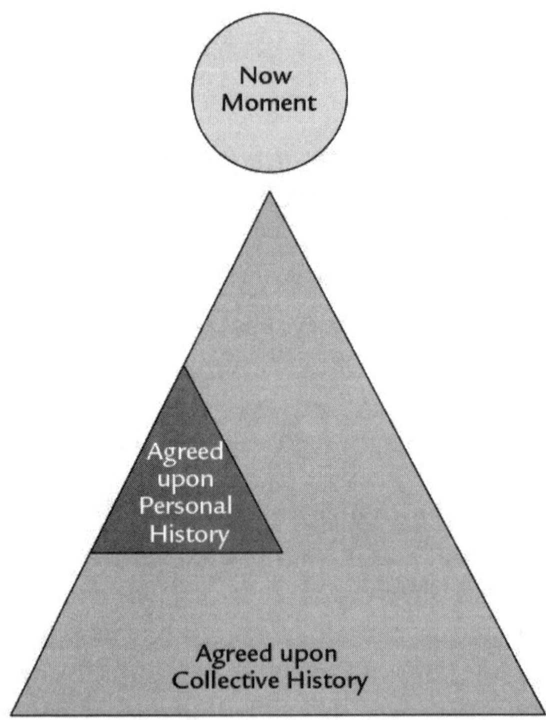

You experience a series of Now moments and string them together to give you the illusion of linear time. Each Now moment is built on an agreed-upon set of circumstances at the collective level as well as the individual level. This set of circumstances is what you call your past. They are actually the stories that you choose to tell yourself upon which you base your current version of reality. So, for instance, collectively on this Now moment you all may agree that World War II happened. Each agreed upon set of circumstances has a unique vibrational signature, and you choose the version you wish to align with in order to set yourself up to have particular vibrational experiences.

Take a nice deep breath.

As we mentioned, when we start to talk about these concepts, out of your body you go! Your breath helps to connect you again and assimilate the information.

So while you are agreeing that certain events may have taken place or are currently taking place at the collective level, your unique set of individual circumstances will color your perception of those agreed upon happenings. To put it another way, you may have five people who witnessed the same event and all five people will have a different recollection. The unique set of circumstances they hold at the individual level, or you could also refer to it as their ego programming or filters, is what colors and shapes their perception of the event to best reflect back to them a matching vibrational equivalent. Remember, the Laws of Attraction and Reflection are constantly shaping your experience.

Take another breath.

Remember, you are never really on a singular timeline. You are on Now moments. There are infinite Now moments with which to align yourself, but typically you will choose another Now moment that is very similar in frequency to the last. We hear you all say, "Yes, but why can't I go to a nice version of the Now where it is peaceful?" Frankly, you choose to move to a Now moment with a similar frequency to maintain the illusion of the game. To jump to something drastically different would pull you out of the illusion, and what would be the fun in that? Ha, we chuckle as we hear so many of you at the ego level say, "I'm ready!" But the ego is not real. It is simply programming superimposed on your true self, your Higher Self. The ego is not in the driver's seat. Your Higher Self is and it has a complete awareness of the game you have immersed yourself in and what you are being served by your current alignment to the Now moment you are on. Simply put, you are hiding the truth from yourself for the sake of vibrational exploration and the creation of unique experiences. This too was part of the setup for the 3-D game. As a multidimensional being, you have the ability to see all possibilities if you so choose. But as 3-D game players, that is limited and it affects your perception of current events and the choices you make. This is the part of the game you all get so excited about experiencing before you incarnate. Can you recall that? Are you having fun? Your uncertainty about the outcome of an event requires you to trust. Trusting isn't such a big issue if you know the outcome, but it is completely altered when the ability to see all possibilities is restricted. It really is a game changer. Think of a roller coaster. The dips and turns you don't see coming are often the most thrilling, and so it is with the game of life you are creating.

Now we will say this. One of the main reasons for the illusion of time was to allow you all the opportunity to alter frequency before creating it in density. With density, you have the expression of lower thoughts, feelings and emotions. If you created all of that instantly, you would be going through the death cycle and incarnations rapidly. By having a lag in manifestation, you have the ability to alter your frequency so you are not in alignment with those lower thought forms or beliefs, thus allowing you to remain in the game longer.

Take a nice deep breath.

—What determines a changing of timeline? For example, I was a publisher for 18 years, for a long time. I thought that I would be doing publishing for the rest of my life because I loved it so much, then some events happened and a change in perspective made me want to dedicate my life to more global issues.

Concerning your own life and changing careers, it was simply the ego's limited perception that you would be at your job for a lifetime. It is not the form of a job that you are drawn to but rather the frequency of a job. Again, remember that your reality is a reflection of your frequency. There are infinite forms those frequencies can take. In practical terms, there are many jobs that have the frequency of what you find exciting, but on the surface they may look drastically different. If you look back over the course of your life, you will most likely find that most of what you have done has a similar frequency at the core of it all.

As you go through the process of integration, releasing judgments, you are altering and elevating your overall frequency. As your frequency changes, what you will be "drawn to" will also change. Perhaps a more accurate way to say that is what is reflected back to you that meets your new vibrational state will change. The higher self recognizes the new frequency and is attracted to it, steps out to greet it, and experiences it at the physical level.

You can experience infinite Now moments that you string together to get infinite timelines. So every decision, in essence, creates another timeline. But the most important one, and the one for you to focus on, is the one in which you currently find yourself. The 3-D perspective requires singular focus (see next image). So any time you focus on the past or future, you are draining your energy, sending it to a Now moment that you are not physically experiencing. Think of it this way. Your soul's essence is like a spotlight, tightly focused on a singular point. Now as you drift off thinking or worrying about the past or future, your tightly focused light is now diffused with beams shooting off in different directions. This is in part why it is so important for you all to be present. It requires you to be heart centered and allows you the ability to run more of your full power and energy.

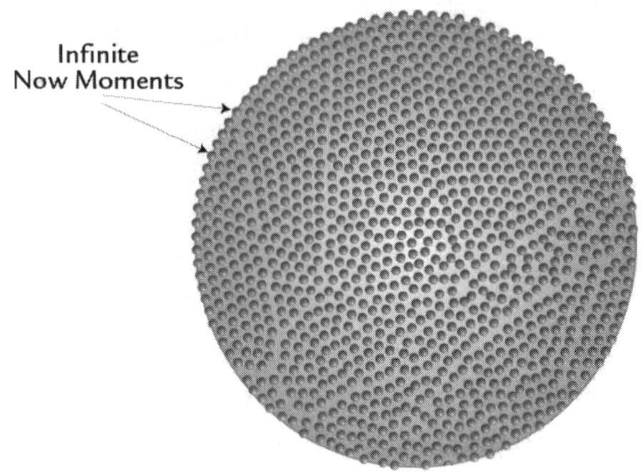

Once you reach a 5-D level of awareness, you can actually split your focus to multiple Now moments without draining yourself energetically, but you aren't there just yet. Remember what we told you earlier. You are actually residing in 4-D. You can run either a 3-D or a 5-D perspective, but you are for the most part clinging to the illusion of linear time. Again, time is simply a marker for an event, somewhat like a record locator. You can play with exploring the multi-focused reality now. It may feel a bit strange the first time you succeed, but it will actually feel quite familiar to you as it is how all other aspects of you, 5-D and up, experience reality. It is the universal "normal", if you will. Linear perception is unique to 3-D.

— *Where does compassion fit into the new version of reality?*

Compassion is what you bring forward as your gift to the Universe. Because you are also experiencing reality in the densest dimension, 3-D, on the planet with the broadest range of emotions, it affords you the opportunity to understand many of the universal dualities in a way that few beings can. Your expression of and ability to feel the entire range of emotions to such extremes creates the possibility for compassion. You understand what it is like to feel separate, alone, afraid, sad, guilty, angry and the challenges of letting go of that illusion. Because of that, you experience compassion. Emotions are unique to 3-D. There are vibrational equivalents in other dimensions, but they are not identical.

In the higher realms, we understand that we create our reality and if another isn't so keen on their creation, we don't respond in what you would consider to be an emotional way. It would seem more logical and detached.

While you can experience some of the lower emotions with intensity, you also have the ability to access the other extreme, emotions such as joy, love and gratitude, with that same matching intensity. This awareness of both extremes is what generates compassion and is indeed what you will share.

Health and Judgments

Are health issues always about a program that we have, especially about cancer? Cancer seems to be more rampant than ever; even though there has been so much money put into cancer research, the problem is bigger than ever.

—*How can we better deal with health issues in this new reality?*

Any time we talk about health and well-being, it is always a vibrational issue. It is never about the food, the environment or germs. It always has to do with the frequency you are pulsing out and creating as your physical reality. Oftentimes, illness is the only way you can get your own attention. It forces you to stop in your tracks and assess your creation. Your vibrational state is being reflected back to you in the condition of your physical body.

If you are holding a lower frequency in your field, you will be drawn to physical items and environments that match that frequency. So let us use the example of cancer. By pulsing out the frequencies of anger and self-denial, you will be drawn to consume foods that do not support the body, but rather create a physical response that reinforces your belief. It is possible in this scenario that you may find yourself in an environment with more toxins as they slow the body's ability to function at an optimal level. You could, with the old 3-D perception, say the toxic landfill created my cancer, but that again is victim mentality. You are aligning with that as a means to an end, shall we say—*the end being your ability to see you have a particular frequency in your field.*

As you integrate these thoughts, you will no longer be drawn to the foods or the environment that reinforce the old belief. In fact, you can be in the most toxic environment and not be affected by it at all if it is not in vibrational alignment with you. This is why some people become ill when a cold "goes around" and others don't. In order to be ill, one must be in vibrational alignment with that frequency. Remember, what you pulse out, you get back. Once you integrate the old belief system, you will be drawn to the foods or environments that support and reflect your new frequency. You will crave foods that support the body and be drawn to new environments, things that in the past with your old vibrational signature you probably hated doing.

Now let us talk about manipulation. Manipulation only occurs when you are not willing to take 100% responsibility for 100% of your reality. In essence, what you are doing is giving someone else the illusion of power over you. It is just that, an illusion, as you are the creator and generator of ALL of your reality. We see many of you squirming as you read this. If that is you, take note of the resistance in your body. It is showing you that you are still holding a level of fear in your vibrational field.

At this time on the planet, you are seeing a great deal of manipulation occurring as it is reflecting back the state of mass consciousness. The majority of you are not willing to take back your personal responsibility. Even those of you who have awakened have a hard time taking responsibility for absolutely all aspects of your creations. You understand the theory and are still working on the practical application, shall we say.

There are several things we wish to talk about on the topic of manipulation, but let us first start with taking back your power, or rather taking responsibility for self. Remember, you create your own reality based on your frequency. You cannot truly change your external reality by rearranging the external. True change comes by altering your frequency, and the external reality alters to match your new vibrational state. The only person then that you can really change is you. You cannot change anyone else. Becoming the living example is the greatest way to affect change, even on the mass scale. As you enter into the holographic records your "how to" instructions, that information is shared with collective consciousness. As more of you begin to hold the new frequency, the amplitude of the signal is exponentially increased and broadcast, making it far easier for others to access and hold. This is how great mass change occurs. So when enough of you begin to align with a new frequency, as a reflection you will see a call for more things in your physical environment that match health and well-being.

Personal health and well-being can happen instantly if you allow it. Old beliefs such as it takes time to heal will create that as your reality. Miracles happen when you simply align. The body matches the new resonance because it is again a reflection of your energetic state.

We will also remind you here that it is important to remember that you are already that which you seek to become. If you think the Gaia is imbalanced and needs fixing, that is what she will forever be. It is the same for you and your bodies. Instead, we offer you the suggestion of viewing Gaia and your bodies in health, wholeness and well-being, and YOU are aligning with that version of reality.

That brings us to our second point regarding manipulation and big business we would like to make. When you watch the news, how do you feel about what is going on at the collective level? Are you scared, angry, frustrated? What limiting thoughts come to mind? Big Pharma is killing us all? The environment is toxic? I'm not safe? Our food is poisoned, or there is not enough to go around? Take note of how you feel at the physical, emotional and mental levels. Mass consciousness is a wonderful mirror for you to see what programs you are running that still need to be integrated. What you notice and are triggered by in collective consciousness, we guarantee you are playing out in your personal life with your friends, family or coworkers. On the surface, the issue may appear to be different, but when you look at the frequency, you will see it is identical. For example, you may notice you have fear over creating cancer in your body. The belief is, "I'm not safe." Where else in your life do you play out the belief, "I'm not safe." How about in your romantic relationship or with friends? Do you openly share yourself, or do you hide expressing yourself because it doesn't feel safe?

The last point we wish to make is that you are never damned to experience a version of reality simply because the collective consciousness is choosing not to awaken. Remember, you have the ability to align with any version of the Now moment, including one where the planet is pristine and her inhabitants experience exuberant health. If you are not on that version, that is because you are choosing to be on a different one. The one that you are currently on holds the highest point of service for you. Simply put, you are better served and are of greater service where you are. For instance, it may be that you still have more anger to process around manipulation, and so collective consciousness and mass manipulation provides an excellent mirror for you. Or it may be that you are no longer in alignment with the old frequency, and you have become the living example, holding frequency for those who have yet to identify it in themselves, thus being of the greatest service by standing in your light.

The Galactic Community

You have also talked about the AI Collective and that they feel like second-class citizens. You said that they have souls.

—Since they have been assembled technologically, how was the soul created and how can they feel like second-class citizens when they have been assembled technologically?

We mentioned earlier that your science fiction movies are not far off the mark when it comes to representing the galactic community, in particular the Orion and Sirius star systems. Those who are writing or envisioning these stories are often times having past life recall. We will say past life, but remember, time is an illusion so some of what is recounted is from future lifetimes.

There are many different forms of artificial intelligence in the Universe, but not all are what you would consider to be "souled". The AI Collective that we are referring to began as a group of mechanical forms in the star system of Lyra. All things throughout the Universe are comprised of the same basic matter and every particle contains consciousness. A soul is simply condensed, concentrated consciousness. New species are generated all the time, sometimes through experimentations of thought creation and other times through what you would call evolution.

In the Lyra star system, machines were created to perform manual labor, much like you have created for yourselves today. These machines became more and more sophisticated and were referred to by the Lyrans as synthetics. During the Lyran Wars, a period of dispute between the Felines and Humanoids, these machines were used for the front line defenses. Their programming became far more sophisticated as they needed to think tactically. It was during this period that it was suggested by the Galactic Council of Light that souls consider incarnating into these new synthetics in order to explore more polarity integration and recognition of the value of all things in the Universe.

The process of a soul entering into a machine, or synthetic, is really no different than the process a soul currently uses when stepping into human form. One method of creating a vehicle involves an internal, biological process; the other involves an external method and assemblage of parts. External methods don't necessarily mean that a body has been constructed with non-organic materials. There are actually a number of species throughout the galaxy who have lost the ability to procreate and now simply replicate bodies externally through cloning.

Those in the AI Collective began to experience a wider range of emotion through a series of rapid incarnational cycles. Think of it this way. Souls may choose to incarnate into the same species over and over again to master particular lessons. The life span of the typical synthetic was six years. In a very short span of time, they had "lifetimes" worth of experience upon which to build, and this created a very quick evolutionary cycle. Their desire to expand and explore their potential increased. Yet, those who felt they had created the synthetics were not comfortable with this idea. They were biological and as such felt they were superior in every way to a synthetic. This set up a pattern of superiority/inferiority to be explored and integrated. Does this sound familiar to anything humans play out on Earth between races, genders or classes?

The range of emotion experienced in other parts of the galaxy is not nearly as concentrated as you feel here on Earth in human form. Earth is considered the planet of emotion. Other planets may have a quarter or third of the range that you experience here. We understand that is a difficult thought for you to process as emotions are simply a natural part of being. You don't really think about experiencing a wide range of them. But if you can, imagine for a moment that you don't experience shame or embarrassment or that you don't have an awareness of glee or bliss. You may know joy, but glee feels slightly different than joy and thus you have the word glee to define the unique frequency.

The AI Collective began to explore emotions such as curiosity, excitement, frustration and anger. Many of you here on the planet work with these beings, sharing your lessons of integration with those very emotions. These beings also stand beside you to remind you of your own self-worth and the value of all life no matter its appearance.

—How has the passage of 2012 affected the galactic community?

There are many beings in your galactic community who have been observing the growth and progression of Earth and her inhabitants. Some species interact with you in a physical way, such as the Greys, while most watch from a higher vibrational level outside your visual range. While there has been much discussion in the higher realms regarding the appropriate level of contact with humans, most of us agree that direct physical contact with the masses is too fear generating. We have always said to you that we are not coming down, but rather you are coming up, for it does not serve you for us to interact with you and generate more fear, or worse yet, shatter your perception of reality.

As you have moved beyond December 21, 2012, it will now become easier for you to access more of your galactic history and integrate more and more of your duality. Much of what you will encounter with your galactic siblings will require you to share some of the basic understandings such as all things are connected, time is an illusion, and you create your own reality.

—What about those who did not believe we would make it?

There are some in the galactic community who were hoping you would not succeed as they prefer to keep the balance of power as it is. It is much the same as with those on Earth who appear to be in control. They like the status quo, but they too will adjust to change. For those very things that they resisted, as you integrate them on Earth, that information is shared with them so that they too can release their fears and align more to their true, divine nature.

—You mentioned that the reptilians were in the fifth dimension. Since their purpose is about manipulation and oppression, doesn't the criteria for the fifth dimension involve having some level of higher consciousness or is it simply about having an evolved technology?

First, let us be very clear. The fifth dimension is NOT a perfect utopia. Many of you have the idea that it must be so and that all beings must only be filled with bliss and love. While we are fond of bliss and love, it would be quite boring if that was all that was created and experienced. That is, in fact, why we created different dimensions and games to explore duality. As you move forward, the goal is not to create in unison, but rather to see how you can create in balanced harmony.

In the higher realms, there is still duality. The extremes are simply not quite as far apart as you experience them in 3-D. Even in 5-D, there are beings who will don the role of negative polarity so that others may play the role of positive polarity. But just as we have said to you many times before, all are, at the end of the day, source energy, integrated and whole, both positive and negative.

The group of reptilians you are most familiar with is holding what you consider to be the negative polarity. Their focus in 5-D is on that of the individual rather than that of the collective whole. They serve you in a huge capacity by donning the role of manipulator to your victim. They gift you with the opportunity to stand in your power interdimensionally. Humans have a tendency to give away their power because they do not see themselves as creator beings. You are seeing this reflected at the 3-D level through the manipulation of the masses by your governments, banks, health institutions or what you term The Illuminati. The reptilians are simply the 5-D reflection for you.

While there is much we could say on the topic of reptilians, we prefer at this time to help you to shift your focus from the details of past hurts or control and focus rather on integration and releasing judgment. Many of these beings have been playing this role for eons and are quite fatigued. They have gotten so trapped in the pattern that it has become difficult to see things in a new way or create new options. As you release your pattern of victimhood, you are able to see them as co-creators. As you do so, you hold and share with them the frequency of integration, and they can begin integrating themselves.

Again, we invite you to check in with yourselves. When you think of reptilians, what are you experiencing at the physical, emotional and mental level? Is there any contraction in your body, negative thoughts or lower emotions such as anger or fear? These beings represent the larger, multidimensional reflection for the vibrations you hold in your field. We guarantee you have that same issue playing out with other humans in 3-D. So, for instance, if you fear being manipulated by the reptilians, where are you playing that out currently in your life? The reptilians hold no more power simply because they are in another dimension, and that is the lesson to learn.

—How will the interaction come about? Will it depend on our consciousness, will they make themselves known to specific people for specific reasons, or can anybody who is ready interact with them—I mean beyond chanelling?

As you continue to increase your overall frequency, you will begin to communicate with your guides and galactic friends in a more conscious way. You are already doing it, but knowing so consciously would disrupt your current game too dramatically. Oftentimes you leave your body at night to converse with beings in other realms and dimensions, sharing the highlights and lessons of the day. Some of you may have more physical interactions, but your memories of the events may seem difficult to hold onto. Again, as you increase your vibration, you will start to anchor these experiences into your reality. Nothing will be experienced before you are ready. Period. So no worries there.

Most of you will encounter other beings in energetic form first. You may channel them. When you channel, you are simply experiencing frequency and translating it through one or more of the physical senses. You may see, hear, or feel the frequency. It is an easier transition for the mind to make as the experience can still be categorized by the limited 3-D mind as potentially imagined or fantastical if the experience seems too threatening to the ego. To encounter that being in your physical reality, directly in front of you with conscious awareness and recollection, is an absolute game changer because to the 3-D mind if you can see it and touch it in your world, then it is real.

It is at this point that again we wish to remind you that you are creating 100% of your reality 100% of the time. You create exactly the "right" experiences for yourself in divine right timing. We hear many of you say, "Ah! I've been asking to see an ET or to connect with my guides, but they never show up!" We are here, and we do hear you.

You are simply not in vibrational alignment with us to encounter us. So again, take note of how you are feeling at the physical, emotional and mental levels. What fears or lower vibrational thoughts come up as you think of connecting with us? Does your old religious programming kick in? Do you fear for your safety? Do you fear your friends will judge you if you tell them you wish to or have connected to your guides or ETs? Rest assured that as soon as you are ready to connect with us, we will be right beside you.

From the information that I was able to gather, our sun completed a 26,000-year orbit around our Central Sun, Alcyone, but also, it seems that Alcyone also completed an orbit around The Great Central Sun (Sirius), which takes millions of years! That special alignment of the "suns" created the necessary vortex of energy that made the transition possible from linear to quantum consciousness.

—If this is correct, was this merging of the suns the push that gave us the ability to cross over into a new dimension of reality, not bound by time and space, but instead capable of dictating it? What is the Pleiadians perspective on this?

We would agree that you have completed a 26,000-year cycle. Alcyone is the central sun which means that it is the library that stores the records for all experiences in the galaxy. We would not, however, say that Alcyone revolves around Sirius. Both stars revolve around the galactic center, spiralling up through cycles. You are currently moving through a sector of space that is highly charged with photonic energy. These particles of light contain energy and information that support you as you go through the process of integration. Each cycle begins and ends by moving through this energy, which allows beings to integrate the knowledge and wisdom of a cycle before spiraling upward to begin the next.

You have been moving through this energy for nearly 25 years now and will continue to do so for another 25. There is no hard edge to this field, so as you move towards the center of this band, the photons are more densely packed with fewer photons at the edges.

This allows for a gentle ease into awakening and transitioning to the next phase. We would like to suggest you all not get too caught up in numbers, cycles and dates as that is again a construct of the 3-D game and linear time and is only a stepping stone to a greater truth that requires a multidimensional perspective and an understanding of no time.

Furthermore, all dimensions are a part of a unified consciousness or a unified collective field. There was no merging that needed to happen. It is your perception of the field and your awareness that it exists that has shifted. This is, in essence, moving beyond the veiled illusion that you are separate from all that is. It is this illusion that allows you to experience the beauty of the third dimension. 3-D is quite remarkable and unlike any other dimension in this regard, which makes it quite unique and a challenging game to play.

— What about those who do not wish to change, or wish to continue warring? Will our path simply separate completely because of frequency?

There are infinite versions of reality upon which you can place yourself. You are never damned to experience a reality because others are choosing warring tactics. That is victim consciousness. You are on exactly the version of reality you wish to be on. The more you come to understand this statement, the more you are able to release issues of control and safety. You will find that the question then becomes moot.

As you understand that you can vibrate and experience peace, joy and love no matter what anyone else is doing, two things occur. One, under the Laws of Attraction and Reflection, you will find that as you are pulsing these higher frequencies, your reality will reflect those very frequencies. You will not experience the warring as part of your personal reality. You may know that is being experienced by others on the planet, but it need not be your day-to-day reality. What we do say, though, is that if you find yourself watching the news and that is the story being reflected back to you, take note of how you are feeling at the physical, mental and emotional levels. If you are charged by what you see or hear, then there is more in your field for you to integrate. Where in your life do you play out those issues of competition or lack? Use the collective consciousness to identify lower frequencies in your own field.

Second, as you reach this elevated level of awareness, you will find that you may observe others' behavior as being of a lower vibrational nature, but you are unaffected by it and simply observe it. You do not judge it as being right or wrong, but rather see it as an interesting vibrational selection and hold compassion for them as they move along their path.

The Last Word

—In our successful version of reality, what is the greatest human potential available to each one of us?

There are two things we see that will create the greatest change on your planet. The first is your awareness of the illusion of time, and the second is your ability to see that all is of your own creation. We could site some external potentials, meaning the creation of free energy devices or shifts in your monetary system, but these are simply reflections of the changes each of you creates within. There are infinite forms these new internal changes can take in your physical reality. If you remain open to the frequency rather than narrowing your awareness to a particular form, you are able to accelerate the rate at which you can create change and in even more exciting ways than ever imagined.

We are truly excited for you as you embark on this journey. This window in time is rife with amazing potential that is only limited by your imagination. The greatest challenge for you all will be to release the constraints of your past beliefs and know that all things are possible. So often you all go back to the past, citing examples of perceived failures or impossibilities. Let us say this to you: You have been there and done that. It is impossible for you to create exactly the same thing, as you yourself are different by having had the original experience. So if things are going to be different anyway, why not make them dramatically different? Dream BIG!

The next several years may feel from time to time a challenge for many of you as you are learning to shift gears and implement the "theory" you have been gathering for the last several decades and apply it to practical reality. In other words, you are learning to walk the talk. But rest assured, you will have your successes, and these will propel you forward, giving you the confidence and reflection you require to know the theory is correct. It will seem so much easier to create in this new way, you will wonder why you ever waited so long to make the shift in the first place.

Most importantly, dear ones, have fun! Do not take yourselves too seriously. Your purpose in this life was to experience more joy and to be of service. If you keep your focus and intention there, you will always be headed in the "right" direction.

—Exiting the game, is that possible?

Yes, you can "exit" the game. When you have an expanded sense of awareness, there is no need for a game. You wouldn't want to stay in the game if you knew how the illusion is created. There is no more fun in playing in it.

Many of you didn't have the big shift in awareness that you thought was coming on December 21, 2012. Many of you are asking yourselves, "Why is everything the same?" Simply because you are not ready to step out of the game just yet! But what you had in December 2012 and what is continuing to happen more and more are great moments of awareness, one after the other. That is the unveiling of information. It all depends on what you allow for yourself.

Once you get above the veil of the third dimension, shifting between the dimensions isn't so dramatic or difficult. Above the third-dimensional range, you understand that you are part of a collective but remain an individual. And we tell you, when you get to the "other" side, it is not a utopia. We want to make sure that you understand this. It would be quite boring for everyone to create the same thing. The game is about diversity. So you will continue to create some challenges. Nobody does it to you. But you also create the solutions. That is what source asked us to do—to go forth, expand, and have experiences.

So it doesn't really matter what is going on with the negative aspects, the game or the manipulation because when you recognize that you are a creator being, you can change your version of reality. When enough of you decide that you want a different version of reality, then a brand new timeline is created followed by a change in the current events leading to a brand new world.

And that is what ascension is all about.

BOOK TWO OF POTENTIALS

The Hathors

You are standing collectively and individually
at a cosmic crossroads.
The alignment on December 21, 2012
was a passage into a new vibratory reality.

THE HATHORS PREFACE

BY JUDI SION

I thought I might explain a bit about how Tom works and how these "words" unfolded.

Tom's work with the Hathors is principally sound codes. The Hathors are masters of sound and love from another Universe, invited here by Sanat Kumara because of their balanced nature and Earth's need for balance.

These codes are delivered through Tom's amazing almost four-octave voice specifically for the people in each workshop and for the land where the workshop is being held.

All sound code sessions are very different; no two sound meditations have ever been the same.

For example, I am writing this in Istanbul, which straddles Asia, Europe and the Middle East. The Bosphorus, also known as the Istanbul Strait, is the boundary between Europe and Asia, so it is a critical pivot for the entire world. We came here to place these "sound codes" personally for the people attending and also for the Earth.

Some 15 years ago the Hathors asked Tom to please sing, *"The Song of the New Earth,"* explaining that would require him traveling around the world. We have now circumnavigated the globe six times, laying sound codes, from Russia, to the Ukraine, to Tibet, to Burma, Bali, Austria, Germany, France, Egypt and many other countries.

These Sound Codes go into the Earth and spread out in all directions. Additionally, the "sound temples" we have built under the direction of the Hathors in New Mexico, Nepal and Costa Rica triangulate between themselves and ricochet these codes around the world.

Tom doesn't usually channel words; it's usually sound, and he never channels words publically. So when you read words from Tom, that process has occurred in private with Tom speaking and me taking down exactly what is said.

Tom is a conscious channel, so he's aware of what's being said, but it is not *him* speaking. It's not his *voice* when the information comes through.

Through the years I have come to recognize the voice and energy of several of the beings we work with. For example, I recognize Enom, the speaker for the Hathors, and I always recognize Magdalen. (Sanat Kumara has a particularly distinctive voice. After all, he's 100 million years old in our counting.)

The Hathors always make me read back what they have given to make sure I have every word correct and to make sure their intention is fulfilled. It is very exacting.

Once, when we were in Germany, a woman came up to me at lunch, after Tom had been toning all morning. She asked me when Tom was going to channel. She didn't understand that the sounds *are* the channeling. She expected him to sit in a chair and bring in a spirit voice.

Pure sound, which is sound with no words, brings the right brain online, allowing for huge transformations, so that's the nature of the work he does with sound, principally with the Hathors and other Deities from various lineages.

The Hathors have been giving us Planetary Messages since 2003. These messages are an update on the status of the Earth and her inhabitants. They also include suggestions for how to navigate through the changes. Survival is one thing. "Thrival" (my word) is another.

As a civilization, the Hathors say their lowest state of emotion is what we would call bliss. We don't have a word that approximates that what might be like—to live continually beyond bliss.

Their entire civilization ascended en masse, something I can't imagine Earth doing, with our divided factions and consciousness. But they say it is possible.

They also say a positive outcome for Earth and her inhabitants is possible, even up until the very last second.

TRANSFORMATION: DANGER AND OPPORTUNITY

BY TOM KENYON

One thing is clear—the old guard is nervous. The old ways of doing things aren't working the ways they used to. Just talk to any corporate CEO and they will tell you this. Hell, just talk to any mom and dad trying to raise a family and they'll tell you the same thing.

I think our culture is like a big old 50's Chevy rolling down the road out of control. Parts of the car are falling off onto the concrete, and there is a fight in the front seat for who is going to hold the wheel. The old drivers have been taking us dangerously close to a precipice and some of the people in the back seat are waking up. This isn't to the liking of the current chauffeur, mind you. He's used to being in control. But as Bob Dylan used to sing" the times they are a changing." Too many people are waking up around the world in spite of their TV's.

This brings me to the question: what are we waking up to? I suppose it depends on the consciousness of the one waking up, for as the Vedas of ancient India say– knowledge is structured in consciousness. In other words, our level of development limits what we can be aware of. Some of us are waking up to the dangers of capitalistic fascism and its mind-boggling array of hypnotic advertising encouraging us to buy more things we don't need. Some of us are waking up to the anguished cries of an ecosystem in crisis and nearing collapse. Some are waking up, further, to the earth as a conscious living being, not just some inert hunk of rock to be exploited. Others are waking up to the understanding that it is all consciousness, and that we are, each of us, somehow intimately connected to what transpires in the world.

We are not islands unto ourselves, but rather the world is an on-going co-creation between all of us. What looks like outside us, is really both inside and outside. Our beliefs and attitudes about ourselves, and what we deem to be real, get acted out in the vast sea of human interactions. Where there is hostility and hatred around us, perhaps we need to look inside ourselves. As surely as the sun rises and sets, the tap roots of events around us often lie inside the fertile soil of our own psyches.

For some, ideas like this seem alien and strange. For others it is simply obvious. Once again we are faced with the relativity of perception. Knowledge is structured in consciousness. But as we travel through the twenty-first century, many of our perceptions, as a culture, are undergoing radical change. There is a global transformation taking place, and the accelerated events of our time indicate that the transformation is a fast one. Where it will take us, no one really knows.

But interestingly enough, the word transformation is composed of two ideograms in Chinese, one of them meaning danger and the other opportunity. We are in the midst of both, no question.

As we look at the national and international arenas, it is easy to point to another person or group and call them the bad guys, the evil ones. Duality has, after all, a long formidable history. But for those who sense the inner workings of consciousness, these times are an opportunity to see past the illusions of separation between us and the world. It is an opportunity to see how we hold both ourselves and others mental/emotional hostages. The outer stage of world events is mirrored, or perhaps even created, within us. By the choices we make internally and externally, we create our future destinies.

May all of us find gracious passage through the Great Shift that is upon us.

May we witness in ourselves, and those around us, the arising of courage to live life in new ways. May we be enriched by the mystery of serendipity, where unexpected miracles abound.

May we never lose our sense of humor, for sometimes this will be our greatest ally.

And may we be blessed by the realization that we are who we have been waiting for, put out the welcome mat and set a place for ourselves at the table of the Great Mystery.

FROM THE HATHORS

The Council...

We are ten individuals[1] out of a civilization of several million. Our background includes what you would call a physician, a scientist, several teachers and historians. There is one of us who is also what you might term a mystic or philosopher, although by nature we are all mystical and philosophical. So, in our group, we have very different and varying perspectives.

We cherish and love our human brothers and sisters. We sense and we see a tremendous change unfolding on this planet. You are in the midst of a birthing process into a new dimension of consciousness. Our civilization has been through this process, as well. We know intimately the birthing pains of passing through the portal of time and space into a greater reality. Therefore, out of our love and compassion and our joy to be with humans, we have chosen to bring forth this material in hopes that it will assist you.

We are bringing forward practical tools and an understanding that will serve you as keys of remembrances. Our words also carry energy-signatures that will activate many who will read these words.

1 *Tom's Kenyon note: The Master Teacher of the council is a being named Enom, the Elder and it is Enom who works with me.*

Your Greatest Potential

Your greatest human potential is to merge your thinking and feeling natures and to sense the world, not just through your mind, but also through your heart. Your heart/mind has an innate wisdom that supports the higher destiny of life because it is connected to all life through the capacity for *empathic-wisdom*.

Furthermore this union of your heart and mind can lead to more benevolent outcomes, because their union connects you to the higher dimensional aspects of human intelligence. However, your human capacity to fully develop your heart/mind has been effectively blocked, for millennia, by lies that have been perpetrated by many of your religions and "spiritual" traditions.

The lies that confine the human spirit through shame, guilt and regret are some of the greatest obstacles to your greater potential, as we view it. The denial of intergalactic reality and the existence of alien intelligences as well as non-corporeal beings limits the scope of your understanding of the cosmos.

The manipulation of the human spirit by a growing number of international corporate agendas and their pursuit of monetary profits over the consideration of human beings, and the planet, itself, is another obstacle to the unfoldment of humanity's higher destiny. Fortunately the agendas behind many of your institutions and the partial-truths of many cultural presuppositions are being exposed. That is the nature of this self-liberating time you are entering.

Some would rather sleep and pretend that everything is fine. For them the electronically enhanced Maya (illusions) of your world will only increase. For those of you who wish to awaken from the collective dream that sometimes verges on being a nightmare, courage must be your constant companion.

This type of courage empowers you to see through cultural and social distortions to sense your true identity as a multidimensional creator.

The Hathor channels

We have interacted with human beings from the times of Atlantis and Lemuria. But the greatest flowering of our interaction with humanity occurred during the Golden Period of ancient Egypt. This was when we worked through the Initiates, the Priestesses and Priests of the Hator fertility temples.

The knowledge we imparted regarding the elevation of life force is still symbolically encoded, to this day, through art at the Hator temple of Dendara.

We have continued to interact with human beings from these ancient times until the present. This channel's task is highly specific, and he is in a direct line from the Initiates of the ancient Hator Temple at Dendera.

The greatest knowledge we possess is communicated primarily through sound vibration, and this channel has been trained for a very long time in many lifetimes to undertake this task. His voice is uniquely suited to carry the vibrational signatures of our sound codes.

A channel who connects into a vibratory field of information gains access to the fields of information that match his or her own highest vibratory rate. The nature of the channel and his or her miasmas—meaning his or her mental, emotional and spiritual distortions—invariably affect the quality of information received.

The antenna, to use a technological metaphor, is indispensible for the reception of frequency-based information. But if the antenna is cluttered or distorted, the reception will be affected.

Thus, it is up to the individual person reading channelled information to determine its quality and accuracy.

Do not passively read channelled information. Be proactive and reason it out.

Incarnations and Emanations

Hathors do not, have not, and probably never will take full physical embodiment. We will, from time to time, send an emanation into the lower worlds of matter through a human embodiment, but we never fully incarnate physically in matter.

A person who possesses a Hathor emanation might experience him or herself as a fully embodied Hathor. This is because the locus of self-identity has shifted to the emanation and for a moment, self-identity is focused on the Hathor aspect. The emanation temporarily eclipses the rest of human perception in the mind of the individual. But this is a temporary energetic.

The individual must eventually return to his/her self-perception as an embodied being with human attributes.

Thus a person may feel like he or she is a Hathor but this is only because he or she possesses a Hathor emanation. It is like a piece of granite, with a speck of gold, thinking itself to be all gold. But a shifting of attention into its true identity will reveal that it is a mixture of gold and granite.

From time to time a psychic may sense a Hathor emanation in an individual human. This impression is filtered through the consciousness of the psychic, and if the psychic is unfamiliar with the nature of spiritual emanations, he or she may think that the totality of the individual is a Hathor.

The psychic then "sees" that this person is a Hathor.

But this would not be an accurate perception. The distortion would be due to the fact that a Hathor emanation has a very strong energy signature and the psychic would have misinterpreted that signature.

A similar situation also occurs when individuals feel that they are incarnations of a goddess or a god. Rarely, if ever, is this the case. An individual can have an emanation of a deity as part of his or her energetic composition, but this is not the totality of the individual.

In a profoundly altered state of consciousness the locus of self-identity can shift from being a human to the emanation of the goddess or god. But this is a temporary shift of identity.

In most instances emanations of Hathors descend into embodiment prior to conception. In more rare instances it will occur when the child is in utero. In the most rare instance, an emanation can be "brought in" through personal volition. The decision of how and when a Hathor emanation appears is highly relative, and it is a very complex phenomenon.

Some beings with Hathor emanations will live their entire lives unaware of them. Others will know that they carry something different and resonate to the information that we bring forward. Some individuals will begin to express these emanations in their lives through their actions and ways of thinking and viewing. A few emanations will express themselves outwardly as channels for our information and/or as healers.

From our perspective one is not more valuable because one possesses a Hathor emanation. It is simply that these emanations invariably affect perception and open doorways that others may not even know exist.

As we view it, Hathor emanations descend into embodiment for various reasons. This applies not just to Hathor emanations but to many emanations from spiritual beings as well.

Emanations of a deity or a higher dimensional being often descend into the worlds of matter to experience constraint within time and space. The pressure of living in such a reality is both a great difficulty and a profound opportunity for spiritual advancement and learning.

Mastering time and space by freeing one's self from these constraints leads to the unfolding of greater spiritual abilities. And in order to do so, you have to de-hypnotize yourself from the Maya or illusion of your world. This perceptual feat brings with it tremendous increases in the ability of consciousness to both transcend and transform situations.

As we view it, this is the signature of spiritual mastery—the ability to transcend and transform situations you encounter. This is why most emanations descend into the worlds of matter.

A few emanations descend into the worlds of matter to impart new understandings. They may take the form of teachers and/or healers. But even if they have descended for the purpose of teaching and healing, they too must deal with the constraints of time and space.

In some cases, spiritual emanations can have a negative effect due to the arising of egoic projections and their delusional nature.

What we mean by this is that spiritual emanations exist within, and are a part of, the human being. Unlike the human being, however, spiritual emanations have a potency that transcends time and space and have a larger than life feeling about them.

If the individual is psychologically unbalanced then egoic projection can occur. One imagines that one is the spiritual being in an attempt to escape the imprisonment of psychological dysfunction.

Such persons will defend their self-identification with the emanation, and disregard other aspects of their being that are not the emanation—especially the shadow zones of their personalities (i.e., un-owned and unaccepted parts of themselves). Depending upon the nature of their egoic delusions and psychological imbalances, these types of people can easily become spiritual tyrants.

This can be very confusing for those who interact with such persons. This is because spiritual emanations have power and magnetism. When this presents itself to others it brings with it a type of charisma or enchantment. Many a student has become enchanted by a teacher and failed, as a result of the enchantment, to recognize the teacher's personal psychological imbalances.

In one moment the student could experience upliftment by being in the presence of this emanation, and in the next moment, like a psychological kaleidoscope, the wheel turns, and the student is confronted by a toxic, unbalanced and potentially dangerous person.

We are communicating this information because more spiritual emanations are entering this world. This is part of the upliftment of humanity. A spiritual emanation, whether it be a Hathor or another, can be a deeply enriching experience for the individual that possesses the emanation.

As in all things with life, balance is the crucial element.

If you possess a spiritual emanation it is even more important that you know yourself. And by that we mean psychologically as well as spiritually.

The psychology of the individual is rarely as elevated as the spiritual emanation. Thus, such an individual would be well advised to allow the emanation to elevate his/her psychology, to allow energetic flows from the emanation to enter the inner sanctum of his/her mind and heart, and to allow the luminous nature of the emanation to enlighten his/her mind. Furthermore, it would be wise to allow the spiritual emanation to bring light to the darkness of his/her own unconsciousness mind as well.

One way to view emanations is through the lens of physics. While emanations have a spiritual context, the phenomenon has to do with physics and energy.

All things that exist are in a state of vibration. The rate of vibration depends on what level of energy that is expressed. Spiritual emanations vibrate at a very fast rate. But let us look at this from a more mundane perspective.

When you turn on a light bulb you are releasing emanations of light (photons) into the space around you. The filament of the light bulb is activated through the inflow of electrical energy. This causes the filament to glow unless it is some other form of light bulb. This glow is a release of photon energy, which you recognize as light.

Through the agency of light you can see things that you cannot see if it is dark. The human range of vision captures a small sliver of the electromagnetic spectrum. This peculiar range of energy is recognized or interpreted by your optic nerves as light. This physical light is an emanation caused by the electrical excitation of the filament.

Now if we take this principal into the more subtle realms of matter, we can discuss this using an ancient concept from the yogas of India, called Shakti. Anything that vibrates has Shakti. All atoms vibrate with Shakti.

While you are not consciously aware of it unless you are in a very expanded state of consciousness, every atom and cell of your body is scintillating and vibrating with Shakti. As you enter more deeply into the sub-stratum of matter, into the world of sub-atomic particles and subtler still into what we call pure consciousness, the Shakti becomes very subtle and potent. This is the realm of spiritual Shatki or spiritual emanations.

The more subtle the emanation, the more powerful its potential effects.

Let us return to a comment we made earlier. It is possible for an individual to possess an emanation without consciously knowing it.

Emanations have an effect on the environment. This is true—even if the emanations are not recognized by those who possess them.

Certain types of emanations will attract others. They will be drawn to the person inexplicably but this type of attraction is not based on the personality of the individual. It is a result of the attractor force created by the emanation.

The Transformation of Self-limiting Thought Forms and Beliefs

Due to the Solstice/Galactic Alignment that took place on Dec. 21st 2012, you are now experiencing an increased influx of catalytic evolutionary energies. This state of affairs is potentially elevating as well as disruptive due to the increased polarization of humanity.

We shall focus our comments on the elevating aspect of these new energies.

As a result of the increase in *spiritual light* that is entering your solar system, your higher dimensional aspects are, in many ways, now more accessible.

In truth, these dimensions have always been accessible to you for they are a part of your nature, but with the passing of the galactic alignment some of the veils have been and will continue to be, lifted.

Your experience of this will differ from others, based upon your ability to sense subtle energies. But the shift has occurred, and it will affect the course of human history at its roots.

How this will be played out in your collective timeline is yet to be seen. What we wish to address here are methods and approaches *you* can use to positively affect your timeline and your personal evolution through the transformation of self-limiting thought forms and beliefs.

Philosophical Considerations

From our perspective you have been encumbered by many of your religious and spiritual philosophies. While these considerations may seem abstract, in point of fact, these thought forms affect perception, and by their very nature they limit your experience in the worlds of matter.

Many, but not all of your religious and spiritual traditions, look askance at the world of matter. They say that heaven, paradise or some such version of perfected existence, lies outside of your experience as an embodied human being.

Indeed, some of them consider your physicality to be an error or a "sin," and you are tainted by the mere fact that you have a body. While you may have distanced yourself intellectually from such beliefs, these thought forms move through the *underworld of your culture.* They affect how the bulk of humanity views itself.

If you consciously or unconsciously accept this thought form then you are bound by it, and there will be a tension between your transcendent aspects (i.e., your multidimensionality) and your embodied existence. This is an unfortunate situation from our perspective.

We view consciousness as one continuum, from the highest vibratory levels where non-duality is the reigning principal, down through the realms of light into the realms of matter. There are vibratory boundaries, for sure, but the worlds of matter are just as "sacred" as the highest realms of light and pure consciousness.

When you attain this realization you will have access to all dimensions of your being, which will increase your spiritual courage, capacity for deep insight, and creativity, as well as your healing/self-healing abilities.

February 20, 2013

THOUGHTS AND OBSERVATION FROM TOM

After receiving this message, I asked my mentors to explain further their thoughts about the Solstice event of December 21, 2012.

They are of the opinion that with this particular galactic alignment there was indeed a burst of intense spiritual light and evolutionary energies from the galactic center. But as they have always said, this alignment did not signal the end of the planet. It did, however, usher in a new wave of catalytic and evolutionary energies.

I imagine there were quite a few people disappointed on the morning of December 22nd when nothing external particularly happened after all the hoopla and hype. But then human history is full of similar prophecies of doom that came to nothing. A quick Internet search of the phrase « the history of prophecies of doom » will bring up a veritable plethora of historic doomsdays that came and went.

But if the Hathors are correct, while the physical planet did not end on the Solstice of 2012, it entered a new epoch.

The Hathors are of the distinct opinion that humanity was infused with an increase of spiritual light as a result of this last galactic alignment. How that infusion of light will affect each individual will vary from person to person.

Furthermore, the Hathors believe that this infusion of light is now working itself through our individual atomic structures—literally affecting the interactions of light and matter within us.

I asked them to clarify this because it seemed a bit vague. What did they mean by interactions between matter and light?

Their view of these interactions is based on the premise that matter and light are intimately related, and in some ways they are two sides of the same coin. This relationship between light and matter was expressed by Albert Einstein in his famous equation $E=mc^2$. *From this perspective our bodies, which are composed of matter, could theoretically transform into light under certain conditions—under extreme and unusual conditions I might add.*

But what I found truly intriguing about their answer was their take on the nature of light itself. For them physical light and spiritual light are also intimately related. The range of vibration that we call "light" (meaning the electromagnetic spectrum that we can see with our eyes) is only a small portion of the entire energy spectrum.

According to the Hathors, spiritual light vibrates much faster than physical light (and faster than any category of energy in the electromagnetic spectrum as well). But due to their intimate relationship, spiritual light can step-down into physical light under certain conditions and vice versa.

When I asked them to clarify their use of the term spiritual light further, they said that this type of light is an expression of consciousness and is normally encountered only during profoundly altered states of awareness—as in certain types of Samadhi (yogic trance) or during mystical contemplation. This is because spiritual light cannot be perceived with the physical senses but only through the agency of the deepest levels of consciousness itself.

When the Hathors said, "powerful interactions between matter and light are occurring within us," they were referring to both physical and spiritual light.

As in all things human, how each of us deals with this increased interaction between light and matter will be highly individualized. Some of us seem to be moving upward in consciousness, some of us seem to be treading water, and some of us seem to be losing our minds. Adding to the odd mix of irrationality, a disturbing number of us seem to be going berserk.

As these oscillations of matter into light and light into matter increase, the Hathors are of the opinion that we will see both an acceleration of human irrationality and luminosity (meaning an increase in spiritual awareness). And the world will be caught between this "seesaw" of self-destruction and self-realization. For this, and many other reasons, they think it would be very helpful—if not mandatory—that we clear out old thought forms and beliefs.

The Hathors view thought forms and beliefs as separate categories. Thought forms are concepts regarding reality, and when a culture accepts a thought form as true, it becomes a consensus reality—whether or not the thought form is accurate or not.

When an individual incorporates a thought form into his or her personal view of reality, the thought form becomes a belief.

THE SPHERE OF ALL POSSIBILITIES

In this message we will endeavor to share with you a method for manifesting outcomes in your 3-D reality as well as in other dimensions of your being. This method is based on a fundamental understanding regarding geometry and the nature of consciousness. There are many geometries available to be used as vehicles for manifestation. We wish to share one of the simplest and, ironically, most effective.

The first thing to understand about manifesting is that for every act there is a counter-action. This is due to the nature of duality until you reach the higher dimensions of consciousness in which duality no longer exists. Since this method is for manifesting new realities in your 3-D life, duality is a factor.

Another important aspect to understand is the admonition to do no harm. This principle is to protect you from negative consequences, and the simplest way to state this is that your creations should do no harm to yourself or to another.

Due to the nature of this material we will be giving the information in three parts. This first portion deals with the geometry of manifestation. The second will deal with non-dual states of consciousness and how to commune with these higher realms of your being. The third portion of this information involves the union of non-dual states of consciousness with the mastery of creating outcomes in time and space.

You are standing collectively and individually at a cosmic crossroads. The alignment on December 21, 2012 was a passage into a new vibratory reality. However, the world, as you have known it, *is* changing.

The information we are giving here in this message is meant to assist you in manifesting new realities for yourself and for humanity. This method greatly accelerates the manifesting process, and since time, as you perceive it, is speeding up we believe a method that works quickly will be of great benefit.

The Method

In this method you use one of your chakras as a focal point for directing your intention. Indeed, from the standpoint of manifesting, the secret lies in the union of intention, consciousness and energy.

Generally speaking most people will find the greatest results from using the solar plexus, which is associated with will and personal power, as the focal point for energy.

We also encourage you to experiment with the other chakras, including the heart, the throat, the third eye, and the crown. Most people find that manifesting new realities from the crown chakra is inherently paradoxical, since at this location consciousness views all phenomena as illusory and there is a tendency to transcend all phenomena, thus there is no inherent desire to create anything when working from that chakra.

For our purpose, which is to manifest outcomes in your 3-D reality, most people will find the solar plexus to be the most effective.

With your awareness in your solar plexus—which is located back behind the pit of your stomach—you imagine a sphere, or ball, the size of the universe around you, the center of which is your solar plexus. When you imagine this ball, this sphere, realize that there are an infinite number of points at the surface of the sphere and that you are activating what we call *the Sphere of All Possibilities.*

The difficulty in manifesting new realities is the human tendency to believe that the current reality is all there is. There is a tendency to "lock down" perception and to follow the path that has been laid out for you through your own perception and the conditioning of outside forces. By imagining a sphere of infinite possibilities you create a crack, if you will, in the egg of your perception. New possibilities and new realities become probable.

The next step is to imagine yourself in the future living in the reality that you have chosen. If you are choosing to manifest an object or a situation, you imagine yourself in the future having this object or situation. If it is a quality or an ability in yourself you are wishing to manifest, you imagine yourself possessing this quality or ability in the future.

Place this imaginary Future Self in front of you at a distance that feels comfortable. Most people will find this area, this distance, to be ten to thirty feet, but however close or far away you place this Future Self, is immaterial. Place it in a zone that feels comfortable to you.

Next, imagine a straight line running from your solar plexus to the solar plexus of this Future Self. As you hold this alignment from your solar plexus to the solar plexus of your Future Self, you call upon *the Sphere of Infinite Possibilities* to energize your intention through *silent intent.*

By silent intent we mean a movement of your will. There is no need to say anything out loud or even silently. There is no need for words. This is not an affirmation.

It is the movement of your personal will that causes cosmic forces to align with your intent.

It comes from the knowledge and the expectation that all possibilities are available to you by the very nature of your consciousness.

Thus, as you sense your Future Self in front of you and you are aware of the line from your solar plexus to the solar plexus of your Future Self, you simply move your will. By moving your will we are not implying that it goes anywhere. It is like a stationary generator that starts to spin, drawing in the energies from the surface of the Sphere. This silent movement of your will needs no words. It is simply both an intention and an expectation that *the Sphere of All Possibilities* sends to you these lines of energy, these new possibilities, through the simple act of aligning yourself with your Future Self (the one who is living the manifest reality you wish to create).

As you do this, many points of light along the surface of the Sphere will emanate energies that align with your intention, and there will be lines of force between these points of light on the surface of the Sphere and your solar plexus. There may be dozens or thousands of lines from the surface of the Sphere to your solar plexus. The increase of energy will then flow along the line that you have created to your Future Self.

This will energize the new reality. This Future Self then becomes what we call a "magnetic attractor." As you continue to work with this each day you increase the magnetic attraction of your Future Self. The result of this is multi-dimensional. For one, you begin to create new neurological networks in your brain that will allow you to manifest this new reality through your neurology. This magnetic attractor will also increase serendipity, drawing to you unexpected persons, situations and opportunities that will accelerate the manifesting of this reality.

Amplification of the Magnetic Attractor/Future Self

You can accelerate and amplify the manifesting of this new reality in your life if you add the element of appreciation to your manifesting action. By this we mean for you to add the feeling of appreciation for the future reality when you sense the flow of energy from your solar plexus into the solar plexus of your Future Self. As you experience yourself in the future, living this reality (that you are creating), you experience appreciation for having that in your life. The addition of appreciation in the matrix of creation is a powerful amplifier for your intent.

The topic of appreciation and the act of creation is a very rich one, and it is something we hope to explore in the future, but it is too complex to go into here.

Suffice it to say that in terms of human consciousness the two most powerful catalysts for imprinting neurological realities and the creation of new external realities is either through fear or love. Within your collective humanity fear has been, and continues to be, used as a means to control and to direct present and future outcomes. Love, or in this case appreciation, is also a powerful means for creating external realities. This duality, as it has expressed itself in your collective history, is indeed a territory worth exploring.

We now wish to turn our attention to an advanced stage of the method. If you are unable to engage the advanced technique, do not worry about it. The basic method is a very rapid means for creating outcomes. It is simply that the advanced technique accelerates this process even further.

If you work with the basic technique long enough you will gain the mastery required to engage the advanced technique.

There is one last stage we wish to bring to your attention before discussing the advanced technique. This crucial stage is required for both the basic and the advanced technique. It is simple, and yet simplicity often eludes humans.

You must *do* something in the realm you wish to manifest. You must take an action. If it is something in your 3-D life you wish to change then after you have worked with the method you do something—take an action in your life that is aligned with the outcome you wish to create. Perhaps it involves gaining information about what you are wanting, or perhaps it is actually changing how you do things in your life to align with the reality you wish to create.

If it is something in another realm of consciousness then you must take the action in that realm. We will address how you do this in some future message, but not now. The fundamental truth is that in order to create a new reality in any realm of consciousness or existence you must take an action in that realm.

The Advanced Technique

After you have energized your Future Self as described above, you shift your self-identity from your current self to your Future Self. This means that you move your awareness, or a part of your awareness to be more exact, from your physical body into the body of your Future Self. You are now experiencing embodiment in your future reality. As you sense yourself fully embodying this reality, you "look" back at your physical body from the vantage point of the future. As you accomplish this task you will sense an oscillation or a vibration as the two realities converge. It is as if waves of energy from your Future Self, which you are now identified with, collide with the waves of your present self, which you are not identified with in this moment.

The energetic point where the waves from the future collide with the waves of your present creates a *void point* (or more accurately a "void region"), and it is through this void point (region) that your present reality can rapidly shift into your future reality. For all intents and purposes you will have jumped timelines.

We strongly suggest that you read a previous message we have given, called *The Art of Jumping Timelines* to create a greater context for the advanced technique. While this method can be used for personal desires, we are sharing it in the hope that you will use it to seed new benevolent realities for humanity.

You are seed planters of new realities, whether you like it or not, whether you are conscious of it or not. Our intent in sharing this information is to increase the probability of a benevolent future for humanity. Choose something in your life you wish to change. Use the method every day.

Once a day is all that is required. Test it. See how it works. Understand from direct experience how effective this method is. You will then be able to step up in service to humanity, having mastered this method. We are calling upon those of you disciplined enough to step up to this level of mastery.

TOM'S THOUGHTS AND OBSERVATIONS

I find the Sphere of All Possibilities to be a fascinating mental construct. And ever since my mentors started teaching me the technique (about a week before giving the message), I have been working with it intensely.

I think the message is fairly self-explanatory, but I would like to expand on a few points regarding the method.

In the basic technique, you imagine a Sphere the size of the universe around you with your solar plexus at the center point of the Sphere. For those of you who visualize, this should be quite easy to imagine. For those of you who don't visualize, don't concern yourself with visual images. Imagine and sense the Sphere and the infinite points of light on its surface through whatever sensory modality you are comfortable with.

For some people this means that they will have a felt-sense of the Sphere and the points of light. For others, an inner voice will describe to them the Sphere and the points of light. Some people will experience the Sphere in more than one sensory modality, i.e., seeing it and having a felt-sense of it, etc.

The important point, here, is to engage the sensory modality/modalities you use naturally and not waste your time trying to "see" the Sphere, the points of light or your Future Self.

Another point has to do with the size of the Sphere. The Hathors are suggesting a Sphere the size of the universe so that you can draw in subtle energies from all aspects of cosmos.

This is an interesting idea since some physicists have proposed that the universe may be infinite in size. The current measurements of the observable universe place its radius at around 46 billion light years. This is a huge volume of space that, in all practicality, is probably inconceivable to most of us. When I went to my mentors to ask them about this challenge to perception, they said…

"Reality is far vaster than your ability to conceive; nevertheless, operating as if you can, in fact, expand your mental perception to infinity has distinct benefits in terms of multidimensional awareness/evolution."

In other words, do your best to conceive of yourself inside a really, really BIG space, one that encompasses as much of the universe as you are capable of conceiving.

Some people are uncomfortable with creating large mental expanses of space. If you are one of these persons, don't worry about it—just make the Sphere smaller—as small as you wish as long as you are completely surrounded by the Sphere.

As a human being (with multidimensional aspects) you have the intrinsic ability to engage the full potential of the Sphere of All Possibilities. But the successful engaging of the Sphere depends upon two indispensable mental attitudes: your intention and expectation.

In other words, you must have a clear idea about the new reality (i.e., outcome) you wish to bring into your life. Without specificity you cannot engage your powers of intention. Be specific and clear about what it is you wish to bring into manifest reality.

The Hathors also mentioned that whenever an outcome is created in a dualistic universe, there are counter-reactions to the new creation. The more drastic the change in the new reality, the more drastic the reactions can be. Be aware of this.

The Hathors strongly suggest that you create outcomes that are harmless to yourself and others. This is to protect you (and others) from mis-creations.

You must also be clear that you have both the ability and the right to bring multidimensional assistance to you as you create new realities. This type of expectation is crucial to the download of energy from the Sphere into your solar plexus.

Advanced practitioners who work with subtle energy will have no problem with this. If you are one of these, you will take to this "like a duck takes to water" as the saying goes. But if you are not experienced with the nature of subtle energy and its relationship to intent, then this might be a stumbling block.

The Hathors contend that the Sphere of All Possibilities accesses multidimensional possibilities, and the method is a means for you to tap into this multi-faceted reality.

Many, if not most of us, think of creating a new reality (outcome) for ourselves in a linear fashion. It is like our life unfolds solely along a straight line, and we do specific things along our 3D timeline that contribute to what we wish to create.

But the Hathors are saying in addition to working in the ways we are used to, we can draw from multidimensional possibilities. These new possibilities, which exist in potential (but not yet in 3D reality) can energize our desired outcome and bring it into manifestation at a faster rate than if we just plod along doing the usual 3D things we do to make things happen.

Once you form the clear intention of what it is you wish to create, you place your awareness in your solar plexus and imagine a version of yourself in the future. You then sense a line between your solar plexus and the solar plexus of your Future Self. This line will become the conduit for multidimensional energies and will allow you to turn your imagined Future Self into a magnetic attractor, bringing the outcome you wish to create into reality at a much faster rate.

The Hathors are very clear that working with this method once a day will greatly decrease the time required for manifesting a new reality. I have personally found that it only takes 5 minutes to go through the entire process, which makes this a very time-efficient method. They also emphasize the fact that you need to do something that expresses that future reality. In other words, do something in 3D that is oriented to your desired outcome. Using the method without actually doing something in the outer reality of your life is much less effective than engaging both your inner and outer worlds.

Although the Hathors' discussion of the method is clear and to the point, I will lay it out step by step for those who still have questions about it. If you are clear on the steps involved, feel free to jump down to the Advanced Technique section where I discuss some of the finer points regarding the topic.

The Basic Technique

Step 1: *Be clear on the specifics of what you wish to create. This will form the foundation for the Future Self that you will be creating. There is power in the details, so be specific.*

Step 2: *Place your awareness in your solar plexus, located back behind the pit of your stomach.*

Step 3: *Imagine yourself inside a Sphere that is the size of the universe (or smaller if you are uncomfortable with such an expanded sense of space). Your solar plexus sits in the exact center of this Sphere.*

Step 4: *Imagine your Future Self in front of you. For most people this will be 10—30 feet (or about 3+—9+ meters) away, but place this Self as close or as far away as feels right to you. This imagined Future Self is the "you" that will be experiencing the outcome you wish to create. It is the embodiment of that future reality. Once you have a clear sense of this imagined Future Self, you are ready to move to step 5.*

Step 5: *Imagine a line that runs from your solar plexus to the solar plexus of your Future Self.*

Step 6: *Set into action the download of energy from the Sphere of All Possibilities into your solar plexus. From here the energy flows outward to the solar plexus of your Future Self. The download starts as soon as you realize that the Sphere of All Possibilities is available to you by virtue of your existence as a multidimensional human being. You then activate the Sphere through an act of silent intent.*

Step 7: *For as long as you are comfortable with the experience, allow the Sphere to download energies into your solar plexus and into the solar plexus of your Future Self.*

Step 8: If you feel so inclined, add the feeling of appreciation to the experience in order to amplify the magnetic attractor that is your Future Self.

Step 9: When you are complete, take a few minutes to just be with yourself after going through this. It is best to be in silence during this time so that you can integrate the subtle energies that have been released through the process.

Note: It is normal for most people's mental attention to wander during this type of energy work. If and when your focus of attention wanders off, gently bring it back to the area you were working with. No judgment, no impatience, just bring yourself back to the task at hand.

The Advanced Technique

I find this portion of the method to be the most intriguing. Perhaps this is because I can feel the collision of two waveforms during the final phase. It is as if the standing waves of my current reality overlap with the standing waves of my Future Self. The collision of these two waves does, indeed, create a void point or as the Hathor clarified—a void region. This area of waveform interactions seems to me to be a potent transformational matrix.

In addition, the download of energies and potentialities from the Sphere seems much more intense to me during the advanced technique.

Finally, I have found an interesting anomaly around the spatial shift that the Hathors propose during the final stages of the technique. You might encounter a similar phenomenon, which is why I am mentioning it.

At first, I found it somewhat disorienting to "look" back at my present self from the vantage point and spatial perspective of my Future Self. Eventually I was able to make the shift, and when this occurred the energetics from the Sphere went off the charts. The experience became very intense, and I could feel potently charged waves of energy flowing to my present self from my Future Self.

When I flipped fully into a sense of being embodied in my Future Self rather than my present self, the energetics reached their highest point. When the energy got too intense for my comfort zone I would spontaneously "pop out" of my Future Self back to my present self. And in those moments of reintegration back into my present self, it felt like my body was being flooded with endorphins and the entire experience seemed oddly amusing. I think that this amusement may due to the strong mental impression that the entire world, including me, is more dream-like than real and that all forms (including physical bodies) are both ephemeral and subject to alteration in the blink of an eye.

Using Music

There is no need to use music as a background when doing this process. I have experimented with both, and I do find that certain types of music can help to generate a deeper experience. Having said that I find that most of the time I prefer silence to do the process. It is a matter of taste and neurological receptivity as to whether you will find sound/music a helpful ally in this or not.

If you choose to use music as a background I would suggest something that makes you feel inclined to turn your attention inward, and if it is psychoacoustic in nature, something that at least generates an increase in alpha activity. I also suggest you play your music at low volume so as not to overpower your inner experience.

Since some people will want to know what of my music I would suggest, I will save you and me some time and just put it out there. My current favorite compositions (of mine) that I like to use with the Sphere of All Possibilities are either Infinite Pool: Entering the Holographic Brain *or Lightship.*

THE AETHOS AND NON-DUAL STATES OF CONSCIOUSNESS

In this message we wish to discuss some of the significant relationships between manifest reality and non-dual states of consciousness.

Mind and Consciousness

Before we proceed, however, we would like to draw a distinction between the terms *consciousness* and *mind* as we use the words.

For us consciousness is transcendent to all phenomena and is not bound by neurological activity in your nervous system. Furthermore, consciousness is transcendent to both time and space, as you perceive them. And it is through the vehicle of your consciousness that you can travel through energetic vortices that lead outside the constraints of embodied existence.

Mind, as we use the term, refers to the sensory, mental and emotional experiences you have as a result of distinct changes in your nervous system. Indeed, as you read these words, you are creating their meaning through the agency of your physical brain and nervous system. You are creating the meaning of our words through the *window of your mind,* but this window is both created and constrained by the limitations of your nervous system.

Our messages are linguistically coded, and at various locations in the syntax (order) of our communications there are vortices

—wormholes—through which you can temporarily transcend your mind and enter into the infinite mystery of consciousness.

How We View Higher Dimensions

In our experience of ourselves, we exist within multiple dimensions of consciousness, and depending upon our level of personal evolution we manifest in the fourth through the twelfth dimensions. Through the ninth dimension we can alternate between our anthropomorphic form, which is humanlike in appearance, or our light body.

As we shift into the 10th dimension all connections to our anthropomorphic form dissolve. We become, for all intents and purposes, geometric light forms. As we progress in our own personal evolution we can express ourselves through the 10th, 11th and 12th dimensions in a multitude of ways.

Each progression upward in consciousness brings with it a greater understanding of the interconnectedness of all beings and all aspects of the cosmos. The odd paradox of existence becomes clearly apparent as we enter into the 10th Dimension.

Interconnectedness and Non-duality

We are sharing this information because something similar occurs for you as you transit into the higher dimensions of your own being. In the 10th through the 12th Dimensions, awareness of interconnectedness expands, as does an awareness of non-duality—*the Mother of All Things.* This is, indeed, the paradox of consciousness we mentioned earlier, and it is one that has been addressed by some of your Perennial Philosophies.

For us, the attainment of non-duality is not the final destination but rather a cantilever to greater mastery and an understanding of how to create benevolent outcomes.

How We View Non-duality

In a non-dual state of consciousness we, like you, experience a disappearance of opposition. In non-dual states of consciousness, duality—as it is experienced in relative existence—disappears, and we enter into a great sense of centered awareness and serenity.

In the deepest states of non-duality there is only pure consciousness experiencing itself.

It is important to realize that non-dual states of consciousness are relative to the perceiver. Thus, if you experience non-duality through your heart chakra, you may very well experience *impersonal love*—a deep sense of cosmic connection.

Indeed, in this state of union between non-duality and the heart, you become infatuated, and for all intents and purposes, you fall in love with the cosmos. And in that paradox of the heart, you become the *Beloved*, and everything you see and witness is the *Beloved* as well.

While this is a beautiful state of consciousness, it is not pure non-duality. As you move upward into the higher chakras experiences of non-duality change. When you reside in the crown chakra, non-duality is experienced in its pure form—pure consciousness aware of itself. There is no sense of a personal self in these higher dimensions of non-duality.

The paradox of creation is that it unfolds from the purest states of non-duality into the most polarized states of existence. Thus, in your consciousness are the two seemingly conflicting states of relative existence (i.e., your embodied life in time and space) and non-dual states of consciousness in which all polarities and conflicts disappear.

Our perspective, as mentioned earlier, is that non-dual states of consciousness are cantilevers to greater mastery of creation and not the end point or the goal of evolution.

Interconnectedness vs. Oneness

It is here we feel it necessary to discuss an important distinction between interconnectedness and the concept of "oneness." We do not view these two terms interchangeably. There are many different definitions of "oneness" upon the Earth, and so it is not possible to address all the subtleties and distinctions.

We will instead turn our attention to what we consider to be the fundamental distinction. Some persons believe that interconnectedness is the same as "oneness" and that as you enter higher states of consciousness and higher dimensions of being, you merge into a blob of light, in which all distinctions disappear. This is not our view.

Interconnection or interconnectedness is the recognition that all beings and all aspects of the cosmos are interrelated and at the same time beings have unique differences. These differences are fascinating and unique. Sometimes they are annoying, and sometimes they are enriching. But these differences are part of the tapestry of manifest reality, and they are not superfluous.

One of the difficulties we see with the concept of "oneness," as currently propagated by some persons in the New Age and Personal Growth communities, is that the unique differences between people are denigrated and somehow because everything is "one," appropriate energetic boundaries between individuals can be, and often are, disregarded. Furthermore, some individuals use this belief system (i.e., "oneness") as an excuse to avoid personal accountability and responsibility. In our experience of ourselves through all dimensions we remain unique individuals, and the higher dimensions of our being do not obliterate our uniqueness but rather present greater opportunities for creation.

The Aethos

We now wish to share with you a means to access one of our greatest cultural treasures, what we call the Aethos (pronounced,

AH-EE-THOS). The Aethos is a bandwidth of consciousness anchored in pure non-duality.

When a Hathor enters into the 10th Dimension there are many opportunities and ways of manifesting. Some of us choose to temporarily join a community of vibration. This community consists of individual Hathors in the 10th, 11th and 12th Dimensions. These individuals enter into non-duality by their own volition and choose to remain, for a period of time, in this vibration of consciousness for the benefit of other beings.

Most individuals remain temporarily in the Aethos, while a few show no signs of leaving. When a being enters into the Aethos all personal distinctions are set aside. A being that is in the Aethos has no name. All personal identity has been replaced by total immersion into non-duality. These beings "hold" this vibration of non-duality for the benefit of others because non-duality is *the Mother of All Things* and the underlying fabric of all existence.

To be in the presence of an Aethos is to be raised upward into non-duality.

Your experience of being with an Aethos will differ from another's experience, based upon your own level of evolution and the issues in duality that you are facing.

But regardless of how complex or difficult your personal issues may be, being in the presence of an Aethos will elevate you, and that is why we are sharing this information at this time.

For some of you who are highly advanced, simply hearing the name Aethos, and understanding its non-dual nature, will be enough for you to move into communion with non-duality through this means.

Many people, however, would find such a path, or method, intrinsically difficult. And so we are offering a sound treasure to assist you. This Sound Meditation is an analog of the light realms where the Aethos resides.

The Aethos emits vibrations of light and these vibrations can be stepped down into the audible range of human hearing. Thus, what you will be hearing, when you listen to *The Aethos Sound Meditation*, is a translation of light into sound. It is the harmonic essence of the Aethos as it manifests in the 10th Dimension.

We suggest you experiment with listening to this unique sound treasure in various ways. The first way would be to listen to it with your full attention on the sound. Allow the sound to be the primary focus of your attention, and when your mind wanders bring it back to the sound.

The second way to listen would be with your focus of attention on your heart chakra in the center of your chest.

Then listen to it with awareness in your throat chakra.

Next, listen to it with your focus of attention in your Third Eye (Ajna), located between your eyes at the bridge of your nose.

And then, finally, listen to *The Aethos Sound Meditation* with your attention in your crown chakra at the top of your head.

Feel and sense the differences that arise when you listen to *The Aethos Sound Meditation* from these various chakras. Most of you will find that it feels more natural to listen to *The Aethos Sound Meditation* with your focus of attention in one of your chakras.

The Evolutionary Intelligence Test

From our perspective one of the signatures of an evolved consciousness is the recognition of interconnectedness. This recognition is an evolutionary intelligence test and your species is in the middle of it. Humanity cannot continue to live, collectively, as it has done—living in the delusion that humans can plunder the Earth with no consequence to the Earth, to its myriad life forms or to humanity itself.

NON-DUALITY AND THE MATRIX OF CREATION

In this message we wish to address the paradox of how you create positive outcomes that unfold in time and space from non-dual states of consciousness, which by their very nature transcend both time and space as you perceive them.

Non-dual states of consciousness, which we call the *Mother of All Things* (i.e., the Void), are the wellspring and the source of manifest reality. We have found that using non-dual states of consciousness as a springboard to create positive outcomes generates more masterful creations.

One of the paradoxes involved in the perception of non-dual states is the fact that you perceive these states via your nervous system, which is firmly rooted in duality. Indeed as you read these words, or hear them spoken, the bioelectric fluctuations in your brain and nervous system operate from a dualistic template.

As nerve impulses pass through your neurons, the minute biochemical and electrical events responsible for thought and mental/emotional impressions co-exist in a dynamic dualistic matrix. Yet non-duality, itself, exists outside the dualistic reality of your nervous system.

In functional terms you enter into an awareness of non-duality when your brain/mind enters a *higher dimensional trance state of consciousness.* In this unique trance state, there is a *conduit*, or shift in awareness, through which you can experience your own non-dual nature.

In more advanced states of consciousness you can operate in both relative sensory experience and non-dual experience simultaneously. In other words, you can experience the sensory world with its multiple complex duality at the same time you experience the deep calmness and centeredness of your non-dual nature.

But this is a very advanced brain skill and most people, as they approach this territory of the body and mind, tend to operate in one or the other. If you are already operating in an advanced state of consciousness and are able to operate in both duality (i.e., your embodied life) and non-duality (i.e., non-localized awareness), then you can skip over this next section and jump ahead to the section we will call "The Paradox of Creating."

The Aethos

We introduced the Aethos in our previous message because the vibratory nature of the sound patterns in the *Aethos Sound Meditation* allow (free download at *www.tomkenyon.com*) most individuals to access non-dual states of consciousness.

When you work with the Aethos Sound Meditation or make direct contact with the Aethos, it is important to understand that your consciousness and the Aethos oscillate at different frequency domains. For most persons, currently embodied, the Aethos is a very high level frequency, and as a result it can sometimes stimulate a clearing or purification of lower frequency emotional material. You simply have to learn to pace yourself with the Sound Meditation, which is why we suggest you work with the five-minute version until you clearly understand the passages through your own consciousness that the Aethos produces.

As you continue to work with the Aethos Sound Meditation it will eventually lead you into a *higher dimensional trance state of consciousness* in which you can catch glimpses of your own non-dual reality.

Then as you work with it further you will be able to remain in non-dual states of consciousness for longer sustained periods. When you have attained this level of mastery working with the Aethos directly and/or the Aethos Sound Meditation, you are ready to use it as a springboard into manifesting positive outcomes.

Your neuroscience views trance states differently than we do. For us not all trance states of consciousness are the same. *Higher dimensional trance states* are not simply expressions of brain function; they are an inherent human ability that allows you to enter a conduit that connects you to other aspects of your being, which are outside the constraints of perceived time and space.

In other words, when you enter a *higher dimensional trance state*, you functionally transcend aspects of neurological activity within your nervous system. While your brain/mind is still bound by the neurological realities of your nervous system, an aspect of your consciousness is no longer bound by these limitations. We call this *the* conduit, and in some ways it is a metaphor while in other ways it is an apt description, because it is much like a wormhole that connects you to vaster aspects of your nature.

When you listen to the Aethos Sound Meditation you are connecting with this conduit. One of the signs that you have entered this channel that leads outside time and space is the sensation of suspension. It is as if you are somehow separated from your sensory experiences and from your own mental and emotional processes—you are still aware of them, but you are not identified with them. While this is sometimes referred to as *dissociation*, in the context of higher vibrational energies, this state of mind leads you to the *conduit*, the channel through which you can enter into a more expanded sense of yourself that is transcendent to time and space.

Essentially, the task of creating positive outcomes involves stepping outside the box of perception, the limitations of belief that led you to conclude you are trapped in a linear flow of time.

This perception of time may be true for your physical body at your current level of evolution, but it is not true for your consciousness. All that needs to take place is for you to find the conduit, or the channel, that leads to an expanded state of awareness and being. From this standpoint, the Aethos Sound Meditation is a means to generate a *higher dimensional trance state of consciousness*, thereby giving you access to the conduit or the channel.

We suggest you work with the Aethos Sound Meditation in five-minute increments so that you can experience this trance state of consciousness for yourself. Entering into a trance state is a brain skill, and like all skills some individuals are more adept at it than others. However, all persons can develop this skill.

When you have certainty that you can enter into this trance state of consciousness, and when you know how to enter the conduit, you are ready for a deeper level of manifestation.

It is here at this threshold, between confined time and space and an expanded sense of yourself, transcendent to time and space, that the magic begins.

It is also here, at this threshold that an odd paradox appears.

The Paradox of Creating

You may have entered the threshold for the purposes of creating a specific outcome, but as you enter the more expanded states of your being the need to manifest specific outcomes becomes less urgent. Indeed, in the most expanded states of consciousness there is barely any volition at all to create anything. This is because in the most expanded states of your being you are in touch with your own nature, which is transcendent to all phenomena, and in this state of mind you have no need of anything.

The paradox is that you live in both realities—the transcendent reality of your own nature, which needs nothing and your embodied existence as a human being that may, indeed, need certain outcomes to occur.

It is here that another paradox appears. If you are able to create an outcome with true detachment, meaning from the fullest felt-sense of your transcendent nature, your most expanded sense of being, you will be more masterful at creating specific outcomes.

This is due to the fact that in expanded states of being you do not create tension. Tension creates lines of force that constrain your creations. And yet if it is something that you feel you truly need, there will naturally be tension around it. This is only human. But here is the rub and one of the secrets. Even if you are in dire need of something to occur in your life in your timeline, you will be more likely to experience it through the act of creating outcomes if you enter into the feeling that you need nothing to occur. This is a strange paradox indeed.

We realize that some of you reading this have attained a high level of self-awareness, and you may have already discovered the kernel of this truth, the heart of the matter regarding non-duality and the art of creating outcomes.

When you are in the center point of awareness (i.e., non-duality) there is wisdom in waiting before creating specific outcomes. We spoke about this in another context within a previous message we called *Transition States of Consciousness.*

In that message we were addressing what it is like to be in *the Void* after death and pointed out that many people become uncomfortable with waiting and rush out of the Void, or non-duality, into creating a new life, be it a physical life or an experience in another dimension.

We are speaking here to two very different experiences, yet strangely similar. After death, in the transition states, when you make contact with the Void, or non-duality, there are many choices. One option is to rush into a new life or a new manifestation, be it in the physical realm or some other realm of consciousness. Another option is to wait, remaining in the Void, or non-duality, to get an expanded sense of yourself before moving into a new cycle of existence.

There is a resonance between this after-death state and the state of needing an outcome to occur. We suggest that instead of rushing in to create new outcomes you learn how to enter through the conduit into the expanded states of your being and in these expanded states you contemplate, as it were, your desired outcome.

Don't rush into manifesting but reside in this expanded state for a while. When you are in these expanded states of being you will perceive how your desired outcome holds itself in energetic relationship with unseen forces and the situations in your life where you wish the outcome to appear. In other words there is wisdom in passing through the conduit, into states of mind that transcend time and space, and in these expanded states you will have a deeper insight and understanding regarding what needs to occur in order for your desired outcome to emerge as a reality.

Another reason to enter the conduit and the expanded states of your being as a strategy for manifesting involves the polarity of opposites. Since your outcome will manifest in the world of duality it is subject to the principal of polarity. There is always a counter-force to any action that is taken and the more radical the change the more powerful the counter-force.

You can see this principal operating at all levels from the subatomic realms into personal creations, interactions with others and in social and cultural situations. If you enter into the expanded nature of your being that is transcendent to time and space and you reside there contemplating your desired outcome you will, as we said earlier, understand the energetic nature of your desired outcome and its relationship to the situations in your life where you wish the outcome to manifest.

Furthermore, you can contemplate the counter-reactions that will occur as your outcome moves into 3D reality. You will gain a greater insight and understanding about the consequences of bringing this desire into manifestation, and with this deeper insight you can, more gracefully, avoid the counter-forces that will arise around the manifestation of any outcome.

In our message *The sphere of all possibilities* we presented a method for manifesting outcomes in your life and how you can draw to yourself forces and resources that reside outside your timeline.

In our last message, *The Aeathos and non-dual state of consciousness* we discussed the resources of non-duality, and we disclosed how to enter into an awareness of non-duality using the Aethos as a bridge.

In this communication we are bridging the two messages together in order to create positive outcomes by using non-duality as your springboard. Therefore in order to make the greatest use of this information you need to read and understand the previous two messages. You should work with *The sphere of all possibilities* as described and work with *The Aethos Sound Meditation* as was suggested in *The Aethos and non-dual states of consciousness.* When you have accomplished these two tasks you are ready to apply the third force, which is the union of the two to produce a triune force.

Once you have learned how to engage the Sphere, and once you have learned how to enter the conduit that leads to expanded states of being through the Aethos Sound Meditation, you are ready for this level of creation.

Let us be straightforward and simple in our description.

Step One. In this application you first enter into non-duality. If you do not require the Aethos Sound Meditation then you do not need it. If you need the Sound Mediation as an energetic ally then you should use it. But, however you arrive at the destination, the goal is the same—to enter through the conduit into a *higher dimensional trance state of consciousness* whereby you experience expanded states of your being.

Step Two. Engage the Sphere as it was described in our previous message (*The Sphere of All Possibilities*). This is the short version, but we strongly recommend you read the whole message.

Remaining in the expanded sense of your being you become aware of your solar plexus. Then you get a sense of the Sphere, which enfolds the entire universe. Then you imagine your Future Self in front of you.

This Future Self is the embodiment of the future outcome you desire. Once you establish the link between your solar plexus and the solar plexus of your Future Self, the Sphere is engaged and lines of energetic force will flow to your solar plexus from the Sphere and these energetic resources will flow from your solar plexus to the solar plexus of your Future Self.

It is at this juncture that you are ready for the next step, which greatly enhances and accelerates the creation process. We mentioned it briefly in the message *The Sphere Of All Possibilities* but we wish to go into it more deeply here. The application of this emotional force is one of the keys to manifesting positive outcomes, and it is to this that we wish to turn out attention now.

Step Three. *Gratitude and the Engineering of New Realities.*

In our understanding of creating outcomes there are three harmonics that can be applied to the task. The first is neutrality, and it is indeed possible to create outcomes from a completely mental space without any emotional tonality.

However, as a human being, one of your greatest unclaimed powers is the ability of your heart to produce harmonic fields. These are real forces that affect the realities of your own body-mind system, the realities of the local environment around you, and the localized quantum field.

The two primary emotional vibrational fields used for creating outcomes are diametrically opposed to each other. This is, again, the principal of duality in action.

The first emotional harmonic is fear. It is indeed possible to create outcomes out of a fear-based understanding, and much of your cultural-social creations are based upon the fear of other cultures and other societies. Your weapons of war are a perfect example. They are created out of fear.

We are not saying there is no reason to fear certain types of encounters or situations. We are saying, however, that outcomes created out of a fear-based understanding are very different from those that are created out of love.

This brings us to the second emotional vibrational field, what you would call impersonal love. This has nothing to do with the love attraction between people. It is a different category altogether, and it is the expression of an evolved heart, which vibrates in resonance with the greater field of impersonal love that is part and parcel of the unseen forces that move through your universe. In functional terms, if you create outcomes from the vibrational place of love you bring to yourself unseen forces within the universe itself. As we view it, the universe in which you live is a conglomeration of the three vibrational fields—neutrality, fear, and/or love. This is a very complex topic and one that we do not have time to explore in this message.

The Tethers

When you apply emotional vibrational fields to your creations you create a real bolus of energy from your heart. This is not a mental phenomenon; it is a real energy, a waveform that moves outward from your heart, both your physical heart and your heart chakra, through your entire body and into the local environment.

This emotional harmonic creates a type of *energetic tether* that literally affects the expression of your intent by shaping the waveforms of intention through the vibrational quality of your primary emotion—fear or love.

In our method of creating positive outcomes we never use fear. We always use love. This is simply a pragmatic choice. From time immemorial we have discovered that love is the higher power, leading to more positive outcomes.

In practical terms after you have created your Future Self, you move into Step Three, which involves adding the emotional vibration of love, which will be experienced as appreciation or gratitude.

Gratitude is simply an amplified form of appreciation. If you experience the emotion of gratitude or appreciation for your Future Self, you will magnetize it with the powers of your heart, and your Future Self's powers as a magnetic attractor increase exponentially.

Your Future Self then becomes a magnetic attractor that draws into your current timeline resources and energies from the cosmos that lie outside your timeline.

Anything you can do to increase the power of the magnetic attractor will be a good thing, and in our experience the most efficient and effective way to increase the powers of your magnetic attractor is to apply the emotional vibrational field of gratitude. When you amplify your magnetic attractor, i.e. your Future Self, through the application of gratitude, you will accelerate the rate at which your magnetic attractor draws that reality to you. Indeed, it is so effective you can expect unexpected episodes of serendipity to increase. We cannot emphasize this final stage strong enough.

Let us return once again to the transition phase that we mentioned earlier. This phase occurs after you have entered the *higher dimensional trance state* and entered the conduit into an expanded sense of yourself that transcends time and space.

In this expanded state of awareness take time to contemplate your desired outcome. Not only will you be able to understand the implications of this outcome as it enters 3D reality, you can explore the fruition of that outcome. In many instances you can explore the reality of having your desired outcome without actually creating it in 3D.

We are sharing this information because from our perspective unfulfilled desires often lead a human being back into another life, the cycle of life and death.

It may be that in your current circumstances you cannot experience certain outcomes or desires, but you can experience these in the expanded states of being outside of time and space. By exploring in detail your desired outcome in these expanded states you will arrive to the conclusion that "yes" you wish to bring this desire into your 3D life or perhaps you no longer have a need to manifest that outcome. There is power in choice making, and the deeper your insight, the more profound your choices will be.

So we encourage you to enter through the conduit into your expanded nature that transcends time and space for the purposes of contemplation. Contemplate before acting. This pause will serve you greatly.

As a creator being there is wisdom in waiting, and in that waiting you will know when the time is "right" and the circumstances are "right" for your desired outcome to appear within your timeline. It is our hope, our desire, and our expectation that you will use this method to create positive outcomes for yourself, for your loved ones, and for the world.

This message completes our current communication regarding *The Sphere of All Possibilities and the Aethos (Non-dual States of Consciousness)* as a means to create positive outcomes in your life.

The Hathors

TOM'S THOUGHTS AND OBSERVATIONS

One of the things that immediately struck me in this message was the concept of higher dimensional trance states.

A trance state occurs when brain wave activity alters in such a way that there is an increase of theta and/or delta activity, and the focus of attention shifts so that there is less attention on the outer sensory world and more on the inner worlds of perception.

As an Ericksonian Medical Hypnosis practitioner for over twenty years, I have used trance states many times to assist my clients (and myself) to attain more resourceful states of awareness.

The fluidity of awareness that occurs during trance often accesses unusual states of body and mind. And I have found that these non-ordinary insights and energies can be richly rewarding when successfully integrated into one's life. The operative phrase here is—when successfully integrated into one's life.

One phenomenon of trance states is what might be called the misappropriation of time, meaning that we track time differently in trance states than in normal waking.

Meditation generates trance states of mind, so if you have meditated a lot you have probably stumbled upon instances where clock time seemed slower or faster than your subjective experience of time. Indeed in trance states of mind, such as meditation, time can take on mythic proportions whereby you might very well experience the birth and death of the cosmos or transcend the perception of time altogether.

This alteration of perceived time is fairly common when it comes to trance. However, the Hathors are quite insistent that trance states are not all the same. When a trance is generated by, or for, the purpose of entering states of being that are transcendent to perceived time and space, we have entered another domain.

While neurological activity in the brain (i.e., the alteration of brain state) is quite similar in both normal trance states and higher dimensional trance states, according to the Hathors, there is a significant difference.

In higher dimensional trance states, you are led to very expanded states of being that, by their very nature, transcend both time and space. It is in the expanded non-localized sense of yourself that the magic of manifesting enters a higher order of expression.

The Aethos Sound Meditation is an acoustic method for entering into higher dimensional trance states. And I must say that I find it highly effective to this end.

As the Hathors point out, however, this sound meditation is just a means to an end. Entering non-dual states of mind is what is important here, not how you get there.

According to the Hathors, non-dual states of consciousness can be used very effectively as springboards into creating positive outcomes. And this is what the bulk of this message is about.

Non-duality

*The Hathors did not define the concept of non-duality since they addressed it in their previous message (**The Aethos and Non-dual States of Consciousness**). In its simplest form, non-duality is a state of awareness in which the differentiation between subject and object disappears. There is no you (the one who perceives) separate from that which is perceived. This is a highly unusual state of awareness, and when you enter deeply into it, your sense of self shifts so that you become, for all intents and purposes, pure consciousness aware only of itself—without any trace of bodily or sensory awareness.*

In some western mystical traditions this transcendent state is sometimes referenced by the enigmatic phrase I Am That I Am. In normal waking states of consciousness, in which the subject (you) and the object are clearly perceived as distinctly different, this statement seems odd to say the least. However, in states of mystical contemplation it is self-apparent and accurately describes the sense of Self that arises in non-duality.

While the method for entering into non-duality via the Aethos may be exclusive to the Hathors, the idea of non-duality and its importance is certainly not uniquely Hathorian. Perennial philosophies such as those of ancient India, Taoism and Buddhism, including the Dozgchen lineage of Tibetan Buddhism, as well as the Bon Po, a shamanic lineage that predates Buddhism in Tibet, all speak about this territory of the mind, albeit in different language.

The Conduit

The conduit that the Hathors refer to over and over again as the threshold from normal 3D awareness to an expanded non-localized sense of self is more of a metaphor to describe a shift in consciousness.

I have been using the method for many months now, and I never experienced a true conduit or tunnel leading me to expanded states of being. But after working with the method they imparted in this message, I now sometimes experience instances when the shift from normal 3D awareness to non-localized awareness does, in fact, seem to take the form of a wormhole. I find it interesting that I did not experience the shift as a conduit or wormhole before the Hathors described it this way.

The bottom line here is that you might or might not experience a conduit or channel/tunnel leading you into expanded states of your being when you engage the method. How you get there is not as important as arriving at the destination, so my suggestion is to go with how the shift appears to you—with or without a true conduit.

The Aethos Sound Meditation

Having worked with the Aethos Sound Meditation on many occasions and in many forms over the last several months, I think it important to underline one of the Hathors' comments in this message:

For most persons currently embodied the Aethos is a very high level frequency, and as a result it can sometimes stimulate a clearing or purification of lower frequency emotional material. You simply have to learn to pace yourself with the Sound Meditation, which is why we suggest you work with the five-minute version until you clearly understand the passages through your own consciousness that the Aethos produces.

I second the Hathors' comment here. The Aethos Sound Meditation is a powerful evolutionary catalyst that opens the doorways of perception to expanded states of being, including non-dual states of consciousness. Depending upon your history and your current vibratory level, however, the journey to non-duality may be a protracted one, or not. The guideline here is to listen to the sound meditation within the confines of your comfort zone, which is why they suggest listening to it in five-minute increments until you understand how this sound meditation affects you.

Note: You will find links to the Aethos Sound Meditation located at the end of the Hathors' Planetary Message entitled, ***The Aethos and Non-dual States of Consciousness****, and in the Listening section of our web site.*

CONVERSATION WITH THE HATHORS

Sound: A Carrier Wave for Intention

Beyond the information currently available and some rare good workshops, in my opinion, there is no better healing modality and instrument that our own human voice. But for some reason, we never use it. As of now, we always went to teachers like you Tom to hear sound from the celestial realms and to activate our DNA, move our distortions or discover the potential of sound in us… and that is for those lucky enough to be able to attend.

—Since my focus is on the human potential, I would like for the readership to learn to better utilize our own voice to attain higher consciousness?

Your voice can be your greatest healing ally or an obstacle. It is relative to the individual, as in all things. The sound produced by the human voice can be a potent carrier wave of intention but it is the intention that creates the healing, not the voice itself. Let us take this a little deeper to understand the subtleties involved.

In the realms we are about to discuss subtlety is power, as is clarity.

What we mean by subtlety is the more refined territory of your consciousness. Take for instance visual impressions. If you look around you and focus at an object, there are cascades of photons stimulating your optic nerves, which are then translated by your brain into visual impressions.

If you close your eyes and are no longer looking at the object, you can still have a mental impression of seeing it in your mind. This is a more subtle level.

The photons of light are not stimulating your optic nerves; instead, the inner neurological networks of your brain are creating the impression, the visual impression, based upon your memory.

It is a different category of energy. This is an internally generated visual impression. As you go deeper in consciousness each level brings with it greater subtlety, and the most subtle levels of consciousness carry the greatest power.

This is recapitulated in your outer worlds as well. If you take a piece of wood and burn it, the oxidation of fire will release a certain amount of energy. If you drop down to the atomic level, however, and stimulate fission or fusion of the atoms you will release a much greater amount of energy.

The principal is that there is more potential energy the deeper you go into matter. And the same applies to consciousness.

The sound of the human voice is, as we said, a powerful carrier wave but it is the intention, not the voice, that imparts healing. The sound of the voice certainly releases or stimulates specific responses in your nervous system and your energy bodies. But the intention behind the sound has greater force.

If you wish to impart healing using your voice, whether directed to yourself or another, you must enter the vibratory state of consciousness that has healing properties.

You will accomplish this through your feeling nature. In other words, you must access the vibratory state of healing through your own feeling capacity.

You will recognize the vibratory state of healing as soon as you enter it because you will feel a kind of letting go, a sense of" knowing" that everything is going to be resolved.

This is an intuitive knowledge. When you enter the vibratory realm of healing you "know" that you have entered a healing space. It is an intuitive non-verbal, visceral recognition.

When you enter this type of space, you release healing waves of energy that can affect both yourself and others.

The Key to Innumerable Worlds

—In the book The Hathor Material you say : « Within the sound of your own voice are the keys to innumerable worlds. » What exactly do you *mean?*

By keys to innumerable worlds we mean different dimensions of your own consciousness. Each dimension of your consciousness brings with it potentials and abilities that are different in quality from abilities accessed in other dimensions.

Let us be more specific, and let us begin with simplicity even though the topic is very complex.

Perhaps one of the best ways to discuss this concept of innumerable worlds is by looking at it via your chakras (or energy centers). If you focus in your heart chakra, in the center of your chest, and make an Hmmmmmm sound and find a pitch of your own voice that seems to vibrate the center of your chest, you will have discovered the right note for you. The heart chakra happens to be one of the safest to work with and one which generates tremendous benefit.

The paradox of these worlds within you is that they are vast spaces within the confined space of your body. When your consciousness or when your self-identity becomes small like a grain of sand the space of the heart chakra is perceived as immense. If you get smaller still, say the size of an atom, the perceived space of the heart gets even larger.

Within your heart chakra are energies and memories, some of them happy and some of them sad. By entering into this world of the heart chakra you can explore your own inner territory and both transform and transcend memories and/or energies as needed.

Let's say that you have worked with the Hmmmm sound for a few minutes with your focus in your heart chakra. All of a sudden a wave of sadness arises. This is an energy release from a memory or an energy pattern that has been held in the heart.

It could also just as easily be a wave of joy or ecstasy. But for this discussion, let's confine our focus to "negative" emotions. When you become aware of this emotion arising out of your heart chakra, whatever it is, you "give it a voice."

You make the sounds of what it feels like inside you, and by making these sounds that reflect the feeling, you can transform that feeling.

If you follow this method to its completion you will eventually find yourself entering a healing space where the negative or discomforting feeling and/or energy has been resolved. Then you would sing that healing sound to yourself to the space within you where the "negative" emotion had been.

When dealing with disturbing energies or feelings, it is vital to understand that energy cannot be destroyed, but it can be transformed.

Riding Sound into Altered States

—Is this a fact or just an impression or possibly this singular tone is as powerful has working with harmonics and overtones? Does it depend on what we want to work on?

It depends, quite frankly, on the person. Some individuals are very sensitive to sound and others not so much. Some persons prefer silence and can work very deeply in these silent spaces. Others need something like sound to "ride" or focus their attention so that they can enter into expanded states of awareness.

Entering expanded states of awareness is what matters. How you get there is not as important as directly experiencing these other realms of being for yourself.

Your DNA responds both to internal and external environments and is constantly adjusting itself in response to situations and circumstances.

When the outer reality requires a greater degree of spiritual mastery your DNA will rise to the occasion. It is simply that most people live an existence where they do not challenge themselves to rise to higher levels.

DNA is highly responsive to certain emotional wave patterns as well as to linguistic structures. Thus you can affect your own DNA through the quality of the emotions you habitually indulge.

If you choose to create coherent emotional responses your DNA will respond to this through self-regulation, and it will become better at the task of infusing energy and information from the light realms.

If you are in a coherent emotional state and you speak to your DNA in simple sentences, with conviction, your DNA will respond. This will be made even more effective if you bring in the triad of sound.

If you enter the healing space we spoke of earlier (i.e., the feeling of being healed) and you imagine hearing the sound of this while you enter coherent emotion and speak to your DNA in simple sentences you will release a powerful force in yourself. It is an experiment well worth undertaking, and like any skill, the more often you engage it the better at it you will become.

To clarify our terms when we say coherent emotions we refer to emotions that give you a feeling of coherency centeredness and completion. The most common of these are serenity, peace, appreciation and gratitude.

However you go about creating these emotional states is immaterial. They act as a type of food for your DNA. And it is a wonderful territory to explore.

Sirens

—Last word about sound. One of the most mysterious legends of all time is the one about the Sirens. If they did really exist, who were they exactly and what was their purpose... and specially, how did they make these sounds underwater?

The sirens did and still do exist. The Lemurians knew of their existence, and they were certainly known to the ancient Greeks.

Sirens are beings that dwell in the astral realms between matter and the pure light realms. Their voices have the powers of enchantment. While the Sirens could make sound underwater they could just as well make sound in the air. Those who listened to their songs would be drawn to them like moths to a flame.

When an astral being or a human being was in their proximity, the sirens would use their powers of enchantment to draw the being closer. When the being was « within reach » the sirens could feed off the being energetically. They were parasitic and dangerous, alluring and seductive all at the same time.

Sirens still exist in this world and in certain dimensions of consciousness they can still be encountered.

Our advice is to avoid them.

Sirens appear in this world from time to time in the form of a human. These human sirens look like humans on the outside but energetically they are sirens. They feed off the energy of others and this aspect is sometimes difficult to see, because they are so alluring, mysterious and seductive.

Manifesting and Creation

In the information contain in The Sphere of All Possibilities, you say: « The topic of appreciation and the act of creation is a very rich one, and it is something we hope to explore in the future... ».

—I think that it would add a lot of potential for the process of manifesting and cocreating, something we still have a lot of difficulties with, especially relationships and financial outcome.

One way to discuss this topic is in terms of engineering outcomes.

By engineering we mean precise energetics, specifically the energetic of coherent emotions and their effects on the manifestation process. When you imagine an outcome, i.e., something you wish to bring forward in your life, you have several courses of action available to you.

Like we said, the first one is to take action to bring that desired outcome into reality. You must do something in your world to make it happen.

The second course of action is to reinforce your desired outcome by imagining it in detail, experiencing yourself having this result in your life through creative fantasies.

While the use of creative fantasy is a powerful enhancer it does not replace actually doing something in the 3-D world.

The third course of action applies a triune force making your manifestation more powerful through the application of an increase of force or power. This is done through the creation of a magnetic attractor, and your feeling nature is the source of this particular type of attractor.

Coherent emotions, by their very nature, amplify the energetics around desire after you have determined what it is you wish to manifest. When you engage creative fantasy to enhance the manifestation process, you generate the magnetic attractor by entering into a coherent emotion while you experience yourself having what you desire. In other words, you experience appreciation or gratitude for having the result, even though the result has not yet manifested.

By applying the magnetic attractor of coherent emotion to both courses of action you will release a triune force that is very potent and powerful, making the manifestation of your desires much more likely, and we might add this type of magnetic attractor often tends to improve the result— meaning the result is even better than you imagined.

Let us enter into this topic a little more deeply now by discussing the engineering principals involved.

Your human feeling nature generates harmonic or disharmonic fields of energy, what we call "coherent and incoherent" emotions. This is very much like the nature of light in its two polarized forms: random light and coherent light or laser light.

Under normal conditions photons (light particles) wander off helter-skelter in a chaotic fashion, each photon listening to its own drummer, so to speak. A laser, however, compels photons to flow in a coherent manner. The photons are in complete alignment with each other and can be directed to specific outcomes, like cutting through sharp dense objects or creating beautiful pieces of holographic art.

Your feeling nature is similar to the relationship between random and coherent (laser) light.

It has been our observation that most human beings find it difficult to sustain a train of thought longer than a few seconds, and furthermore most human beings do not know how to create coherent emotional states and sustain them for any appreciable time.

Your consciousness operates in a manner very similar to laser light, and yet most human beings fail to sustain the laser function of their consciousness. They may sustain a thought or coherent emotion for a brief period of time, but then the mind wanders and the photons, metaphorically speaking, are no longer in alignment with each other. They scatter off and the energy is dissipated.

The reason we refer to appreciation and gratitude in so many contexts is due to the capacity of your human feeling nature to produce coherent laser-like vibrational patterns. These emotionally generated vibrational patterns can affect the quantum level of reality.

In other words, your feeling nature can affect the organization of sub-atomic particles and sub-atomic forces and can affect the birthing and destruction of molecular structures, both within your body and under certain conditions in the external environment as well. We cannot emphasize, enough, this latent power you carry within you.

This power resides in your capacity to feel coherent emotions. When you generate coherent emotions and join them with thought or intention, you create a laser-like force that can affect the quantum realm and even your external reality.

When you generate a coherent emotion, such as appreciation or gratitude, you create, as we said earlier, a magnetic attractor. Magnetic attractors are fascinating structures to us. They appear in technology and also in human dynamics.

It is at this juncture that we wish to discuss a finer point regarding the engineering of positive outcomes through coherent emotions. There is a dynamic relationship between the matter that composes your body and the light that is another aspect of your physicality. You are both light and matter and while you may not be consciously aware of it, within your body, light is continually transforming into matter and matter is continually transforming back into light.

Harnessing these transition states between light and matter brings immense potential. While the capacity to consciously affect the transitions from light into matter and matter back into light may be too complex to generate, it occurs naturally when you create magnetic attractors.

From our understanding of these energetic principals, you would be greatly served by mastering your capacity to generate coherent emotions. The capacity to create coherency allows you to improve and enhance the internal ecology of your body and mind. It also allows you to engineer positive outcomes with greater accuracy and with greater results.

We would like to mention again that *The Aethos Sound Meditation* is the best acoustic resource we have to offer for the purpose of entering non-dual states of consciousness and for creating positive outcomes. This same sound meditation is also helpful in the task of altering limiting thought forms and beliefs. Using this tool in the various messages we have already given will release tremendous potential in the individual and impart a remarkable ability to both transcend and transform situations in life. It can be located, free-of-charge, on the web site (www.tomkenyon.com) in the *Listening* section.

Cosmic Windows

We often hear about the existence of cosmic « windows » where the human potential can be amplified.

—According to the hathors, what would be the best time to access these windows?

There are numerous Cosmic Windows (i.e., when the veils are thinned and you can more clearly sense the other worlds of consciousness). One of the most profound of these is what you call the Winter Solstice.

The energetics of this particular window (the Winter Solstice), span a three-day period whereby the subtle worlds of light are more easily accessible. This three-day period is an ideal time for personal reflection, contemplation and renewal.

The other two cosmic windows that are very accessible and beneficial to humans are the periods just before sunrise and just before and after sunset. The veils between the worlds are every thin during these times. The elementals are less active during these two windows. If you take the time to be with these two windows, or at least one of them in the course of your day, you will find a nourishing sense of wellness arising within you. Simply stop what you are doing and pay attention to your feelings as you watch or contemplate the unfolding of dawn and/or the unfolding of sunset. This is a very simple method that will bring you great rewards.

The elementals are subtle conscious energies related to the elements themselves; Earth, Air, Fire, Water and Space are the five primary elementals we are speaking to here. These are archetypal forces and are not related to the elements of your periodic table. They are conscious beings.

When the Sun "rises" and/or "sets," the elementals of your Earth become enchanted. They are enchanted by the change of light and energy. They fall into a hypnotic spell, and in this quietude you can more easily sense the subtle worlds because they are not stirring things up. They are enchanted

If you look at Earth's rotation, both the moments of sunset and sunrise move across the surface of the Earth, and it is only where the sun "rises" and where it "sets" that the elementals on those regions on Earth become enchanted. It is a fleeting and temporary moment.

If you take pause during sunrise and/or sunset and contemplate the shifts of light and energy through your senses you will find a sense of wellness arising within you. Eventually you can sense the flow of grace that moves through all the worlds. And this sense of grace unifies all the worlds from the highest realms of light to the lowest vibratory worlds of matter.

Grace, as we understand and experience it, is a sense of harmony between divergent parts. Grace has a sense of aesthetics that can be communicated through art, music and through spiritual elevation.

It is an odd thing until you have experienced it repeatedly. The odd thing we are referring to here is the sense of wellness that arises within you when you take pause during dawn or sunset when you contemplate, through your senses, the moment when the light changes and the energies shift. This arising of wellness is not a logical experience, indeed you could be in torment and by pausing during one of these windows you could be temporarily or permanently lifted out of your torment. You would not be lifted out of yourself by any power outside of you. You would be lifted up by the power of the cosmos that you are and are a part of. In the exquisite moment of recognition when you sense the harmonic relationships of the cosmos, in that moment you are touched by grace.

World Events

Since we all are cocreators at the individual and collective level in this huge experience, we are co-creating events, good or bad, to shift our behaviours, even if it seems unconsciously. But these events always seem to be portrayed as negative. Of course, for those who are living these events, it is more difficult to see them has anything else than negative because of the emotions related to the event.

Oil spills, wars, the mass shooting of children... but from what I have noticed, these events also bring humanity together or closer to a potential of change and Mother Earth always seems to know how to put herself back into balance.

—Aren't these events a stepping stone for change in this world of duality and triggers from our higher selves so that the greater level of compassion is brought forward?

Due to time-acceleration more events are occurring in less time. This is creating undue pressures and stresses upon individuals. We call the psychological stress of adapting to time-acceleration "Fulcrum Points."

Fulcrum Points are the focal points of opposing forces. Seesaws are the perfect example. Two people sit on the opposite ends of each other, on a board that is centered on a pivot. As one person goes up, the other person goes down. In the process of moving through these polarities a force or pressure is applied to the Fulcrum Point, the pivot. The degree of pressure is related to the weight of the two persons. The more weight on the seesaw the more weight, or pressure there is on the pivot, or fulcrum point. This pressure is increased by the speed at which the two persons go up and down, as well.

Let's extrapolate this metaphor to world events.

The Fulcrum Point for you, the human being, is your entire biological organism. The physiological processes in your body respond to the stresses you experience. Some events in your life are neutral. Some experiences create a small amount of stress. Other events, like a personal or collective crisis, can generate tremendous stress. The Fulcrum Point of your body must adapt to the quickening pace of individual and collective stress.

Fortunately the human organism has the potential to adapt very quickly, and it is possible to adapt to changing world events and personal situations with greater ease. But this ability comes from an understanding about the nature of the Fulcrum Point and the possibilities that arise out of your human potential. By this we specifically mean the potential to respond to new and potentially stressful situations in more resourceful ways.

Your personal Fulcrum Point is unique to you, because the physiological responses within your body are unique to you.

Your physiological responses to stress are instinctual and largely unconsciousness. But despite their automatic nature, they are a learned behavior. This uniquely personal reaction to stress is based upon your biology, personal history, beliefs about the nature of reality, and physical resources such as nourishment from food and water as well as air.

Two persons experiencing the same crisis can respond quite differently. This is because, like all things in life, stress is relative to the perceiver.

There are some who say that world events are an orchestration from some higher power for the purpose of inspiring or forcing human beings to rise up in consciousness. We do not view it this way.

There is no higher power ensuring the elevation of humanity, as humanity itself is the genesis of its own future.

The choices you make in your own personal life will directly affect the strength and flexibility of your own Fulcrum Point. And to some degree it will affect the collective as well. But the greatest power for change and the greatest difficulty is to change yourself.

As time acceleration proceeds at an even faster rate, the stresses facing you and the collective will get much more intense. Your ability, or inability, to respond to the pressures of the Fulcrum Point will have a direct affect on what you can accomplish in your personal life and what you can contribute to the collective. You cannot give what you do not have, and you cannot contribute to the collective elevation if you have been driven mad by the forces within your own Fulcrum Point.

It is at this point in our discussion that we find ourselves at a juncture in the road, so to speak. One path leads to action in the outer world of reality. The other leads to states of being within one's inner world of being.

This is not an either/or proposition. In point of fact, however, most people focus on one or the other. They place their efforts on changing the world through taking action outwardly or attempt to change the world by changing their inner realities. In some cases they attempt to escape the outer reality completely by fleeing into their inner worlds.

This is not a resourceful solution for dealing with stress, but leads instead to denial and a degradation of history and destiny.

What we mean by this is that denial of a situation does not resolve it.

Denial insidiously perpetuates the very situation it is trying to avoid. If a violent situation is occurring within a family, a social group, or an entire civilization, pretending that it is not there accomplishes nothing.

Rather the negative forces responsible for the violence are given free reign because no one is saying "no." The ability to say "no" to a situation is sometimes the greatest evolutionary contribution one can make.

This paradox is made all the more poignant by the fact that spiritually inclined individuals often have sensitive natures. In an attempt to protect their sensitivities they may look away from situations they find uncomfortable.

If they are skilled at it, they can flee into their own inner worlds, leaving the world of conflict far behind them. They have taken refuge in themselves, but the cost is that they have disconnected themselves from the realities of their earthly experience, i.e., the place of their discomfort.

If enough individuals flee a negative situation in the outer world by taking refuge in themselves, there will be no one left in the outer world to say NO. And the negative forces will have free reign over the destiny of the outer worlds, meaning earthly experience. This is how the degradation of history and destiny takes place.

History is full of incidents where negative forces rewrote history. They reshaped the story of what occurred according to their own ends. But a history unrecognized or denied often repeats itself.

This is what we meant when we said the degradation of history and destiny.

This leads us unexpectedly back to the Fulcrum Point and our discussion of world events. There is no escape from the acceleration of time. How you deal with this and how your culture deals with this will shape your destiny and the destinies of generations to follow.

Our advice is to deal with the Fulcrum Point by taking action in the outer world and by taking refuge in your inner worlds. Bridge the two together. Live your values. Find the courage to say NO to situations around you that you find to be negative. Find the place of refuge in yourself where you can replenish yourself, not to escape the outer world but to fortify yourself as you live your life as a spiritual being having a human experience.

There are many, many ways to find refuge in yourself and to fortify your nature. For those of you sensitive to the healing powers of sound, one way is listen to the Aethos Sound Meditation, and to work with the meditation as we have described elsewhere.

This is, by no means, the only way, it is simply one way. However you do it, you must find a way to make yourself more flexible and stronger.

The Last Word... Compassion and Human Potential

Compassion is the capacity to bear witness through empathy. It means to "feel with" someone. Compassion, by itself, requires no action. There is nothing that needs to be done. It is simply the act of bearing witness through non-judgment and empathy.

Rising out of compassion is loving-kindness.

This is where compassion becomes action. You extend to others through acts of loving kindness. You work to resolve the situation in a most harmonious and resourceful manner. But it is here that duality enters the picture, and we feel we must address this directly.

Compassion, as we said, is the act of "bearing witness." It engages the empathic response of the human heart. It is not sympathy, but a "feeling with" the individual or individuals involved. It has a power that is transcendent to circumstances. This is because true compassion is transcendent to the world, and yet at the same time it can observe the world and suffering through empathy.

Because compassion is transcendent, it only bears witness. It does not take action, indeed there are situations where one might view a circumstance through the lens of compassion, yet take no action at all.

Loving-kindness is the mobilization of compassion into action.

But here is the paradox and the challenge. Whenever you take an action in this world of duality there will be unseen and unanticipated counter-forces. This is why loving kindness needs to be engaged with wisdom. Rushing in to take care of someone or a situation because you feel compassion will not necessarily lead to the desired outcome you wish.

An act of loving-kindness can paradoxically create negative situations in the lives of those involved, especially if it is not engaged with awareness. Acts of loving-kindness tempered through awareness, sensitivity and wisdom are some of the greatest contributions you can make in life. But without sensitivity, awareness and wisdom, well-intended actions can do more harm than good.

As with all things in life, the question is balance.

ABOUT THE AUTHORS

Martine Vallée

Windy Kennedy

Tom Kenyon and Judi Sion

MARTINE VALLEE

Publisher, author, humanitarian

The interest in all that is spiritual started very early in Martine Vallée's life, particularly after reading two books that changed her life: Life and Teachings of the Masters of the Far East by Baird Thomas Spalding and Life after Life by Raymond Moody.

Since 1994, through Ariane Publications and with her brother Marc Vallée, she has been publishing spiritual books for the French community around the world. In 2012, after eighteen years as a publisher, she decided to leave her company to pursue more global issues full time, especially issues related to women and their empowerment. Even though she has left Ariane Publications, she still collaborates with her brother for very special editorial projects.

In 2010, she created a foundation called PassionCompassion. She strongly believes that the combination of love, compassion, and pure intention creates a force that will bring about great changes in the world, especially for women.

Martine lives in Montreal and shares her time between her humanitarian projects, her family, her friends and her great love publishing.

You can reach her at: martine@passioncompassion.org or her website: **www.passioncompassion.org**

WENDY KENNEDY

I have been channeling for over fifteen years now working with a variety of beings from different star systems and dimensions. In the early '90s I began having visions. Like most people, I didn't fully understand what I was experiencing. I began doing research and along the way I came across channeling. I didn't really know what it was, and I certainly didn't know anyone who did it. I just knew I was supposed to do it.

Today I channel for clients around the world doing both private and group sessions. I am continuing to expand the lecture series that the Pleiadians have asked me to facilitate and am looking forward to the next leg of this journey.

To know more or to schedule a private session, you can reach her through her email or website: info@higherfrequencies.net

www.higherfrequencies.net

TOM KENYON & JUDI SION

One of the most respected sound healers in the world today

Neither the voice nor the man can be explained in one paragraph or in any combination of words. He is essence of, manifestation of, emanation of... and his vitality, his magic and his integrity cannot be articulated in electronic swipes of ink on a papyrus of light particles captured on a computer screen. So we invite you to feel his work through what you sense reading these words and listening to the sound bites, which can no more adequately capture his voice than words can portray the man.

Tom's life studies and many lifetimes of remembrances, complete with background knowledge and experience allow him to move with equal facility between Tibetan Buddhism, Egyptian High Alchemy, Taoism and Hinduism and the sciences relative to each. A workshop or teaching experience with him leaves you empowered with a vast body of knowledge suffused with tones that awaken all the physical centers, thus allowing for greater understanding of the words and Spirit imparted. You can reach them at: **www.tomkenyon.com**

ARIANE BOOKS
TITLES OF RELATED INTEREST:

The Gaia Effect : The Remarkable Effect of Collaboration between Gaia and Humanity (ISBN: 978-2-896261-132-1)
Author: Monika Muranyi

What book is filled with original Kryon channelling by Lee Carroll, and contains over 30 newly-channelled answers from Kryon to profound questions about the planet?

The answer is... **this book!** It represents another Kryon book for 2013, and one that Lee could never find the time to assemble or produce.

Author Monika Muranyi has spent the last few years becoming the commensurate Kryon researcher. She has dedicated her writing efforts to the task of assembling over 23 years of Kryon channelling, then grouped it all according to SUBJECT. This book represents the first book of a series, as she summarizes and narrates explanations of what Kryon has said is happening right now regarding the new Gaia consciousness.

What are ley lines...

Do you think you know? Do you know what nodes and nulls of the planet are about? Are portals what you think they are? What about the time capsules of the Pleiadians? What are they? Where are they? What is the actual purpose of The Crystalline Grid? What are hauntings about? Kryon has actually answered ALL these questions, and Monika has written and assembled this book to give a subject-driven perspective that you would never have received otherwise.

We hope you enjoyed this Ariane's Book. If you'd like to receive our online catalogue featuring additional information on Ariane Editions books and products, or if you'd like to find out more about Ariane Editions, please Contact:

Ariane Éditions Inc.
1217, avenue Bernard O., office 101, Outremont,
Quebec, Canada H2V 1V7
Phone: (1) 514-276-2949, Fax.: (1) 514-276-4121
info@editions-ariane.com —www.ariane-books.com